The tragedy of enlightenment

An essay on the Frankfurt School

Cambridge Studies in the History and Theory of Politics

EDITORS

Maurice Cowling
G. R. Elton
E. Kedourie
J. C. A. Pocock
J. R. Pole
Walter Ullmann

The tragedy of enlightenment

AN ESSAY ON THE FRANKFURT SCHOOL

PAUL CONNERTON

Cambridge University Press

CAMBRIDGE
LONDON   NEW YORK   NEW ROCHELLE
MELBOURNE   SYDNEY

Published by the Press Syndicate of the University of Cambridge
The Pitt Building, Trumpington Street, Cambridge CB2 1RP
32 East 57th Street, New York, NY 10022, USA
296 Beaconsfield Parade, Middle Park, Melbourne 3206, Australia

First published 1980

Set, printed and bound in Great Britain by
Fakenham Press Limited, Fakenham, Norfolk

Library of Congress Cataloguing in Publication Data

Connerton, Paul.
The tragedy of enlightenment.

Includes bibliographical references and index.
1. Frankfurt school of sociology. I. Title.
HM24.C653   301'.01   79–16102

ISBN 0 521 22842 5 hard covers
ISBN 0 521 29675 7 paperback

FOR ROBERT AND ANTHEA

CONTENTS

PREFACE

Any inflated expectations which might be fleetingly aroused
in the prospective reader by the title of this book should be
promptly modified by its subtitle. What follows is an essay
on Critical Theory. This is subject to three intentional limitations.

It is important, first of all, to distinguish between Critical
Theory as understood here and the Frankfurt School in a more
general sense. The Institute for Social Research, which was
founded in Frankfurt in 1923 and came under the Directorship of
Max Horkheimer in 1930, was notable, particularly during its
early years, for its ability to accommodate scholars of significantly
varying political persuasions; and among these a number were
actively engaged in left-wing politics. Wittfogel, Grossmann and
Neumann were cases in point. Wittfogel was for a time a member of
the Communist Party, before he later became a fanatical anti-
communist and assisted the Congressional committees of the
immediate post-war period. Grossmann was an economist of
orthodox Marxist persuasion, whose continuing political
commitment led him after the war to return to East Germany to
take a Chair of Economics at the University of Leipzig. And
Neumann was an active member of the German Socialist Party
until it was suppressed by the National Socialists, and worked until
the very end as a lawyer for socialist trade unions. These facts are of
more than biographical importance; the Institute for Social
Research is interesting, as an organisation, partly because of the
diversity of responses among its members to the problems con-
fronting twentieth-century Marxism. But Critical Theory, as
understood in the following essay, does not refer to this organisational phenomenon, except indirectly. It refers to a set of concerns

which, I shall argue, are to be found in four thinkers – Horkheimer, Adorno, Marcuse and Habermas.

In the second place, the essay focuses on the time-span between the crisis of the early thirties and the temporary equilibrium of the late sixties. The justification for the opening date is self-evident: it marks the point at which Horkheimer began systematically to redirect the research work of the Institute. The opening of the seventies is, as yet, less clear as a turning-point. Nonetheless, it is then that Habermas left Frankfurt for the Max-Planck-Institut in Starnberg, where he has established around himself a group of younger scholars whose collaborative efforts may well turn out, in time, to mark as substantial a reorientation as that which followed upon the assumption of the Directorship of the Institute at Frankfurt by Horkheimer in 1930. However that may be, the chronological limits set to the terrain covered here means that a number of Habermas' recent works are not considered here. These include not only his *Legitimation Crisis in Late Capitalism*, but also his lengthy debate with Luhmann in *Theorie der Gesellschaft oder Sozialtechnologie*, and his subsequent study, *Zur Rekonstruktion des historischen Materialismus*. Any critical judgements passed in the following essay cannot, therefore, be taken as prejudging this more recent work.

Finally, and most important of all, this is not an epistemological study. At least two of the thinkers here considered – Adorno and Habermas – would want their work to be taken seriously as epistemologies, and they are fully justified in making that claim: no study of their work which sought comprehensiveness could afford to neglect this aspect of their writings. But important works have already appeared which undertake the critical dissection of precisely these problems, problems which are in any case beyond the competence of the present writer.

This essay sets out to ask in relation to each of the thinkers generally considered most representative of Critical Theory what they mean by critique, and it seeks to convey an overall sense of the continuities and discontinuities in their investigations. This is done mainly by highlighting two key issues: partly, by setting their answers in the context of certain cultural conventions of German intellectual history; and partly, by studying the ways in which their critiques illuminate the historically changing character of the public world.

I am grateful to Karl Acham, Graham Bartram and Geoffrey

Hawthorn, all of whom made valuable criticisms of an earlier version of this essay. I would also like to thank Dermot Fenlon, for his generous moral support to a writer en marge de la société: and the Social Science Research Council and the Trustees of the Leverhulme Foundation for grants which substantially assisted in the completion of this work. Finally, I wish to thank Mary Fuller and Hazel Hedge for cheerfully producing excellent typescripts.

Paul Connerton
Cambridge 1978

ABBREVIATIONS

DA   M. Horkheimer and T. W. Adorno,
Dialektik der Aufklärung
(Frankfurt 1969)

DE   M. Horkheimer and T. W. Adorno,
Dialectic of Enlightenment,
trans. J. Cumming
(London 1973)

KT   M. Horkheimer, *Kritische Theorie*,
2 vols, ed. A. Schmidt
(Frankfurt 1968)

1

Introduction

Anyone who sets out to write about Critical Theory should acknowledge at the outset the pitfalls which lie in his path. Access to the proposed object of study is impeded by difficulties at several levels; and it is as well to begin by disentangling these into their separable elements. There are at least three possible layers of resistance. The first is a matter of historical accident: it concerns the availability of the writings in question, as this has been affected by the vicissitudes of German history. The second is intrinsic to the writings: their relative inaccessibility cannot be accounted for solely by a series of accidents, since difficulty is inscribed in the language of the texts themselves. And the third concerns the meanings clustered within the concept of critique: for these can be understood only within the framework of certain cultural conventions specific to German intellectual history.

The first of these difficulties, the literal availability of the writings, is at first sight a relatively straightforward matter. The pertinent facts may by now be assumed to be well known. Critical theory, although a creation of the early thirties, was also a discovery of the late sixties. In the intervening period the body of work associated with it had become difficult of access. Although the institutional base of critical theory, the Institute for Social Research, had been reconstituted – after enforced exile in the United States – in connection with the University of Frankfurt in 1949, there is a sense in which the return of the exiles occurred later. The Institute's journal, the *Zeitschrift für Sozialforschung*, which had continued to appear mostly in German until the outbreak of the Second World War, but which subsequently became difficult of access, was republished in its entirety in 1970. A two-volume edition of some of Benjamin's writings had appeared only in 1955, fifteen years after his death. Early work by Horkheimer and Marcuse surfaced again with essay collections like *Kritische Theorie* and *Negations* in 1968. And *Dialektik der Aufklärung*, which had provoked little reaction when it first appeared in 1947, was republished in 1969.

Critical theory enjoyed more than recuperation in the late six-ties. By that time, the tradition was being renewed by a second, post-war generation. Rediscovery and rejuvenation have moved forward together. Most prominent, of course, is the work of Jürgen Habermas. At this stage, he is not only the most important expo-nent of critical theory but also its representative figure: critical theory now received attention by winning a new dimension of publicity, not simply through the fact of publication and re-publication. One of the most notable features of this renaissance has been a readiness for open public debate with representative figures outside the tradition. Habermas' investigations have opened out into an arc of inquiries. These include the debate with Popper and Albert in the 'Methodenstreit';[1] with representatives of the German student movement;[2] with the philosophical an-thropology of Gehlen;[3] with the philosophical hermeneutics of Gadamer;[4] and with the systems theory of Luhmann.[5] This open-ing out is also a reaching back. At least in the first of these disputes – but surely not there alone – the repercussions of the thirties continue to be felt; the 'Methodenstreit' of the sixties' documents, among other things, an intellectual and spiritual crisis brought about by the collapse of German liberalism in 1933 and the still latent fear of a resurgence of totalitarianism in a new, perhaps smoother, guise.

For the notoriety of critical theory during the sixties an immedi-ate explanation lies ready to hand. While post-war France pro-duced the anti-novel, post-war Germany produced the anti-public. During its opening phase, the West German Protest Movement encountered the combined effect exercised by the quite manifest force of the police and the more covert force of the media. Not surprisingly, the writings of men like Horkheimer, Adorno and Marcuse were resorted to in order, partly, to justify the practice of a counter-movement. The anti-institutional elements contained within the reanimation of critical theory formed a significant part of the attempt to attack what was seen as the compulsive force of a commodity-dominated society, and to do so through the explicit politicisation of repressed interests and needs. Negatively, this meant the breaking down of the elaborate apparatus deployed by an advanced productive process for the deferral and repression of instinctual drives. Positively, it meant an attempt to establish a real directness: to understand and if possible surpass the separation between 'the world as experienced' and 'the world as communicated'. Plundered editions of Horkheimer and Adorno, linked to the establishment of autonomous methods of publishing and distribution, may be seen as part of a general effort to set up a 'counter-public', independent of the official publishing system, and, to that degree also, independent of the prevailing productive process. There was, in short, a felt need to set up an autonomous public world.[6] But the need contained powerful anarchic elements. In that sense, the fascination exerted by critical theory during this period may be described as a kind of sudden uprush from the unconscious, driving against the overwhelmingly conservative carapace of the Federal Republic. Given the forces at work, it is hardly surprising that the function fulfilled by critical theory within the West German Protest Movement gave rise to historical errors at once painful and productive. Horkheimer and Adorno, in evident ways by then politically unradical, were schematically identified by many of their students with the rather more Marxist leanings of the original Frankfurt Institute for Social Research, founded in 1924; with their politically more radical former colleague, Marcuse; and with their – Horkheimer's and Adorno's – own, apparently more radical past.[7]

It is back into the past that the inquiry must be pressed, if the reanimation of critical theory is to be understood; its revival was not simply the return of the exiled, but the return of the repressed. The programme of a critical theory of society, as sketched out in the thirties, had placed those who subscribed to it in a marginal situation for half a century.

Their marginality predated their enforced exile. For they were pursuing studies which had been virtually crushed out of the sphere of official public recognition in Germany. Long before the Institute for Social Research was established at Frankfurt in 1924 – before 1870, in fact – political science had been taught in German universities. But that had come to an end with the establishment and consolidation of the German Empire. Yielding to the pressure of the Iron Chancellor, the German liberals abdicated their political role. Political and social scientists – precisely those who might be expected to be concerned with the reform of politics and society

– were no longer trained in German universities. Two great intellectual bulwarks, already in existence, were deployed against the emerging challenge of Marxism and social science: jurisprudence and historicism. In jurisprudence the focus was on the authoritarian element – the *Obrigkeitsstaat* – and on the legal element – the *Rechtsstaat*. German liberals now concentrated on the *Rechtsstaat* theory. But this meant that the origin, the creation, of law was no longer a concern of theory; legal theoreticians confined themselves solely to the definition of the rights of the citizens, especially his property rights, against the state.[8] Meanwhile, historicism had become the last religion of the educated. Practitioners like Droysen and Dilthey, reinforced by the Neo-Kantianism of Windelband and Rickert, traced historical developments back to the personal motives of individual statesmen and other outstanding personalities; or to the religious attitudes of specific social groups, as in the discussion over the origins of capitalism. When not handing out accolades to 'great men', historians screened off the crass discontinuities of the political world by raising them into the sublime sphere of 'spiritual' developments. With his integration of political history and history of ideas Meinecke brought this strategy to its culmination. Talking about history in the language of 'individuality', 'development' and 'organic growth', he wove a fine network of imagery belonging to the age of Brahms when scholars had been able to bring their thoughts to fruition with the aid of drawing rooms, pianos and private gardens. By 1933 this world was rapidly fading away with the andante. By contrast, the research of the Frankfurt School, located outside the conventional university context and aimed directly at understanding the fact of fascism, was more zeitgemäss. Hence their rapidly enforced exile to the United States.

They were marginal in exile. Their position was an unsettled one both administratively and intellectually. Administratively, because their flight from the heartland of Europe could no longer be like the emigrations of the eighteenth and nineteenth centuries, when 'uprooted' intellectuals – a Marx, a Herzen, a Bakunin – roamed more or less freely. There had occurred a change in the status of the intellectual and in his social environment. This had been brought about by the emergence of the nation-state and the advance of rationality. The bureaucratisation of society brought with it, as one of its aspects, the tendency for the intellectual to be transformed systematically into a functionary of society. The members of the Frankfurt School remained acutely aware of the dangers of this liberal absorption into a 'steel-hard shell': the threat that the contemporary intelligentsia could be turned into defenders of the status quo. While parrying this threat, they were living intellectually between continents. It is true that, despite its scope, the *Zeitschrift für Sozialforschung* retained a degree of cohesion by steering between two extreme positions which at that time typified the relationship between philosophy and the social sciences. One pole, embodied in their German heritage, was respectful of theory and history, and contemptuous of empiricism and pragmatism; the other was represented by the almost exclusively empirical orientation of the social research being done in the United States at that time. It is also true that their critique of mass culture and of the potential for authoritarianism in American society made a substantial impact on intellectual life in the United States, just as the experience of modern American capitalism was to some degree reflected upon by the critical theory. But through an impediment of language the tradition was only partially assimilated in the new world. This was a self-imposed impediment in the interest of a virtual future: in an attempt to retain links with a national culture then threatened with annihilation, the *Zeitschrift* continued to appear mostly in German until the outbreak of war.

Their marginality continued, even if diminished, after the period of exile. For in returning to their homeland men like Horkheimer, Adorno and Pollock were once more putting themselves in an unusual position.[9] Only a few exiled scholars chose to return to Germany, in spite of the fact that the material and nonmaterial rewards of German universities at that time were, on the whole, greater than in the United States. But those who did return home brought with them what they had learned from an alien culture. The collective researches of the Institute now began to appear in a score of volumes in the series *Frankfurter Beiträge zur Soziologie*, in which the experience and partial assimilation of American society and of American sociology are manifest. Thus the *Frankfurter Beiträge* moved forward, modulated, from the projects begun in the *Zeitschrift*. This placed the main exponent of critical theory in a paradoxical situation. While in exile they had combated the over-enthusiasm for empirical research, and stressed the need for historically-oriented theory construction, in the Federal Republic they became, necessarily, advocates of empirical social science.

In the sixties, those who had lived on the margins came to

occupy the centre of the stage. It would probably be wrong to attribute the new clamour for these works solely to the rising temperature of the late sixties, associated among other things with the revival of German Marxism and the international student movement. The import of this bunching of events around the year 1968 reaches back much further. It has to do with a particular kind of discontinuity in the historical process itself. The relationships between the generations in history are naturally difficult, and fraught with pain: modern German history is a searing instance. With the benefit of distance in time and space, it is possible to see more clearly something of what was happening in Germany during the late forties – at the time, that is, when the Institute for Social Research was being reconstituted in Frankfurt.

Too much had happened too quickly. The political unification of the German nation, completed only in 1871, was reinforced by a powerful state bureaucracy, but remained unqualified by the traditions of political liberalism enjoyed by her Western neighbours: even the German term for the public sphere – 'Öffentlichkeit' – was a late borrowing from the English 'public' and the French 'publique'. Nationhood was rapidly followed by capitalistic industrialisation – a process that occurred later, more rapidly, and through the operation of more concentrated entrepreneurial and state agencies than was the case in any other Western nation. The sheer tempo of the process posed enormous problems of adaptation. Or rather: difficulties arose not so much from tempo alone as from the co-existence of different temporalities. On the rapid road to a technical–scientific civilisation German society suffered the co-existence of many contradictory social elements, distinguishable social formations at different stages of maturity – what one writer has called the 'simultaneity of the unsimultaneous'.[10] And then again the German nation underwent three political traumas in the course of twenty-seven years: the collapse of 1918, the collapse of 1933, the collapse of 1945.

By the time of the third and greatest of these catastrophes, the 'Zusammenbruch' of 1945, a syncopation of suffering had been set in motion whose reverberations echo on. Men tried to blot out the sound of the syncopation with the thud and hammer of building. Frantic rebuilding enabled them to forget, until they were more ready for the work of remembrance. The stunned defence against the danger of sinking into collective melancholy left the task of true mourning still to be done. An economic miracle was quickly achieved, but there was still unfinished business back home. Post-war Germany was a society without fathers, whether through disownment or through death.

In the decade immediately following the collapse of the Third Reich, the inhabitants of the Federal Republic turned away from the study of their history. Their national past and their historical thinking had fallen into discredit together. The results were evident in the work of historians and sociologists. Among historians there was a widespread, and acknowledged, 'wearinesss with history', a willed amnesia, an inclination to treat the previous thirty years as if that had been a period during which they had not actually lived. German historians were simply not yet prepared to set that epoch within the perspective of a more or less continuous national history. More important than this temporary taboo on historical thought – a taboo which lasted until about the mid-fifties – was the fact that the catastrophes of recent European history had shattered the last remnants of faith in 'History' as a process with an immanent meaning, a unity and a direction: for how could such an image survive the extermination of six million Jews? The interim taboo on historical thinking, and the erosion of the characteristically German preoccupation with philosophies of history, left a vacuum.[11] For a time this was filled by the fascination exerted on German scholars by American social science. Of course, many of the conditions which had fostered the growth of American sociology, whether empirical studies or Grand Theory – neither of which are notable for their sensitivity to the facts of tragic waste – were lacking in Western Germany. Nonetheless, the sociologists of the Federal Republic were strongly drawn to empirical social science during the fifties and sixties. New research techniques, which held out the promise of 'ethical neutrality' and 'rationality', were seized upon: with their aid, it was hoped, traditional social prejudices might at last be demolished and a practical contribution made towards the promotion of a more rational, and more liberal, form of political life.

But this access of enlightened optimism was an import from a younger culture. It was difficult for it to take firm root in German soil or to provide a proper focus for re-thinking European memories. The means of spiritual recuperation were indigenous, and took longer to mature.

This work of remembrance had begun before 1945 and it continues still. Between 1934 and 1943, the classicist Schadewaldt meditated on the world of the Homeric epics, reviewing, among its many aspects, the journey of Odysseus through the Land of the Dead. These studies, published in Leipzig in 1944, were shortly to be followed in 1947 by Thomas Mann's variations on the Faust theme, a historical allegory composed at a safer distance from the scenes of slaughter. And much later there are residues of roughened bitterness to be found in the novels of Gunther Grass, and a more compassionately ironical coming-to-terms in the fiction of Heinrich Böll. At about the time when Grass's novels began to appear, some German historians were turning towards a new kind of political history, in which they sought to assess the recent past critically, often with the explicit aim of contributing to the development of a new, democratic society. Initially centred on National Socialism and the Weimar Republic, their attention later extended back to the imperialistic tradition in German history. In the mid-fifties Ludwig Dehio and Gerhard Ritter fought their duel over the role of militarism in German history; and the publication of Fritz Fischer's *Griff nach der Weltmacht* in 1961 – the same year, incidentally, in which the confrontation of Popper and Adorno opened the 'Methodenstreit' among German sociologists[12] – unleashed an embittered discussion on the subject of German political strategy before and during the First World War. On a calmer note the psychoanalysts Alexander and Margarete Mitscherlich explored some peculiarities in the psychic economy of post-war Germany in *Die Unfähigkeit zu trauern*. They wished to explain why it was that, even in the mid-sixties, the Third Reich and the collapse of the Weimar Republic had received scant critical attention. This was not of course to cast aspersions on the efforts of those historians whose expertise had recently been trained on precisely those areas; it was rather an attempt to explain the defective diffusion of that work among the public at large. For in practice, the Mitscherlichs argued, the behaviour of the German people as a whole was still determined by unconscious denials of their past. And they suggested that there was an intrinsic connection between, on the one hand, the tone of social and political immobilism then characteristic of the Federal Republic, and, on the other, the stubborn maintenance of a well-organised inner resistance, an affective block, against events of the past which were charged with guilt and therefore 'denied'. But if this could be said of public behaviour – the turbulence of 1967–69 suggests qualifications on this score[13] – a counter-movement was at work.

Heidegger's studies in philosophical hermeneutics were being assimilated and elaborated by a number of German philosophers and theologians during the sixties and seventies. Philosophers like Gadamer, Apel and Lohmann, and theologians like Bultmann, Ebeling and Pannenberg were reflecting on the relationship between traditions and their interpreters. This modern hermeneutic movement may be viewed, in one of its aspects, as the work of mourning. In the field of hermeneutics, as in those of psychoanalysis, historiography, the novel and elsewhere, many writers were trying to come to terms with the German past – to remove bandages from the eyes of their countrymen.

For the wounds lay very deep. In 1945 there was no authority left in Germany who remained uncompromised. Other than a vague hope in European integration, it was impossible to cleave to any political concept which might have issued from a resistance movement against Nazism. The problem was not only one of wide public scope; it was an internal difficulty. For millions of Germans the loss of the 'Führer' was not the loss of a person; connected to the image of that person were powerful identifications which had fulfilled a fundamental function in the lives of his supporters. He had embodied their own ego-ideal. As such, he had been invested with a high degree of libidinal energy. The collapse of 1945 brought the loss of this object; the German ego-ideal had lost its real prop. More than that: the leader was rapidly disclosed by the victors as the arch-criminal. With this sudden reversal in the qualities ascribed to the ego-ideal, the ego of every implicated individual must have experienced a crucial depreciation. When this impoverishment was reinforced by a newly effective 'conscience', whose tangible power was represented by the victorious opponents and their apparatus of retributive justice, new mechanisms of self-defence were necessary. The fear of retaliation and the feeling of worthlessness had to be parried. For the preconditions for a collective retreat into depression were abounding.

Yet the Federal Republic does not seem to have shown signs of any such general depression. Those who had lost their leader and found their homeland occupied and in ruins soon discovered a strategy for evading the devaluation of themselves. They sought to break off all affective bridges linking them to a past which lay immediately behind them. They withdrew emotional energies from events which related directly to the criminal acts of the Third Reich, its enthusiasm, its idealisation of the Führer. This withdrawal of affective energy should not be seen so much as a conscious decision but rather as something which developed unconsciously: the psychically willed disappearance of previously exciting events from the memory. By such means the seemingly insuperable threat posed by the loss of self-esteem was overcome. A past given over to liquidation had itself to be liquidated.

But, of course, at a price. Insight into the overwhelming burden of guilt was held at a distance by three reaction-formations – responses which overlapped, yet also developed, one out of the other. First of all, in response to the corpses in the concentration camps, the disappearance of the German army, the news of millions of Jews, Poles and Russians killed, there was an extraordinary numbness of feeling. No flower can grow on snow. In the frozen rigidity of this turning away, the past had to be impoverished anew by withdrawing from it the preparedness for all pleasurable or unpleasurable participation; it became unreal, dreamlike. That made it possible, in a second phase, to avert the disoriented daze and identify with the victors without too much indication of wounded pride. And that, in time, made possible a third phase: now energy was directed with an almost manic exclusiveness to the physical rebuilding of industrial potential. This reinforced the rewards for the psychic, not only the political economy: the past was subjected to a 'Verfremdungseffekt'.[14]

The work of remembrance, in hermeneutics, in historiography, in the novel, may be viewed as the long and painful breaking down of these defences. The communal work of mourning was an answer to the collective act of self-estrangement. If critical theory was being assimilated during the same period, that too was part of the same complex of circumstances. Its sudden notoriety arose not simply from its mere availability; it was the return of the repressed, its acknowledgement. So that if many of the writings of critical theory sound atonal to Anglo-Saxon ears, that is in some degree due to the fact that their notes formed part of what for the English-speaking world was an alien melée of sound. But their part was a particular one. For much of their work set out to interpret the facts of totalitarian domination; while their continued existence, as a recognisable tradition, remained a witness to the capacity to endure such circumstances, as well as interpret them. The institutional base for critical theory, the Institute for Social Research at Frankfurt, was the only collective, institutionalised representative of the Weimar Republic in the Federal Republic; and it was thus able to offer a special area of mediation between past and present, a thread of spiritual continuity. Thus it was that the caesura of the Nazi period itself fostered the renaissance of the half-submerged tradition. The dispersion of catastrophe could be made to yield one form of recuperation.

The reception of critical theory, it can be seen, is a story of impeded assimilation and belated acknowledgement. Yet the problem of accessibility cannot be accounted for solely by a series of accidents. It is not a matter of circumstances alone. In part at least the relative inaccessibility of the Frankfurt School is intrinsic to it. The difficulty is inscribed in the language of the texts themselves. Here we arrive at the second layer of resistance in the study of critical theory.

This applies especially to the work of Adorno, Benjamin and Habermas. Of the three, Adorno was perhaps the most mercurial and phenomenally brilliant; whereas Benjamin and Habermas convey reverence and a sense of gravity. What they all share is an intense seriousness and a sustained element of attention; and, with this, an explicit awareness of the intimate bond linking the substance of an argument and the mode of its presentation. For all of them language is far more than the 'form' in which their 'content' is transmitted. It is the constitutive medium which informs content and from which content can in no way be detached. They may sometimes be too self-conscious in their use of language; but they certainly do not mince their words.

These writers therefore constitute by their existence a powerful plea for the importance of difficulty.

Adorno was a musician manqué. He was a man of abundant, bursting energy and fertile imagination; mercurial, voracious, histrionic. In what repelled him, as in what drew him on, he was a man of extremes. Opponents he sought to trap by pincer-movements, catching them in the cauldron fire of his arguments; while Nature appeared to him with an equivocal face, at once smiling and terrifying. From this issued a tragically cerebral relentlessness, shot through with mordant irony, in his analysis of the contemporary cultural situation. So it was fortunate that he found in Horkheimer a friend of sounder diplomacy who stood by him for many years; by complementing him, Horkheimer helped to give him a passport to existence. During this time Adorno composed many works of range and force. He contributed to *Authoritarian*

Personality,[15] the major concern of which was with the potentially fascistic individual, one whose psychic structure is such as to render him particularly susceptible to antidemocratic propaganda. Adorno's essays in this collective undertaking show an understanding of the sado-masochistic collusions by which authoritarian posturing can descend, as by a law of gravity, to bestial violations: here he explored the primordial modes of relationship to others which live on, and sometimes even predominate, in the lives of adults. In *Philosophie der neuen Musik*[16] he dealt largely with Schönberg and the twelve-tone technique; he professed his conviction of Schönberg's commanding importance, and then proceeded to subject the system to searching criticism. He was active in promoting radical modern music; yet his radicalism was accompanied by an intense feeling for tradition. Indeed, his technical mastery of the whole body of Western classical music was enormous. An American singer who worked with him said that 'He knows every note in the world'; and Thomas Mann – who received the benefit of his expertise while composing *Doctor Faustus* – called him his 'Privy Councillor'.[17] And in works like *Noten zur Literatur*[18] he considered a wide range of literary problems in their philosophical and sociological implications. He wrote on his peers and contemporaries – Sartre and Lukács, Benjamin and Bloch, Proust, Valéry, Thomas Mann and Beckett; he pondered the achievements of some earlier writers – Goethe, Balzac, Heine, Hölderlin; and he meditated on more general problems of literary form and convention – on the epic and on surrealism, on the standpoint of the narrator in contemporary society, on lyricism, and on the disappearance of the semi-colon in the twentieth century. He always took great pains over his writings: their total shape, their interstices, and the finest details and nuances of their composition. The literary form perhaps best suited to his sensibility was the essay. He inclined innately towards small forms: the aperçu, the fragment, the aphorism. Even a few pages of such writings can certainly not be read at one sitting; they demand episodic reading. Some of his aphorisms in *Minima Moralia*[19] are astonishing: they really knock you back. His often epigrammatic power drew much – though not all – of its forcefulness from a felt need for the integrity of things, a sense of their specific uniqueness, a cherishing and a partisanship of the individual, of that which is not or cannot or simply will not be 'integrated', whose whole nature resists systematic form. So it is hardly surprising if he was a notoriously difficult writer to read. He meant to be. Some of his sentences were long, others short. They were by turns complex and 'blitzartig'; they have torsion and jerk. They contain the power of propositional astringency and acoustic sensuousness. His long sentences are architectonic, containing masterful craft and vehement pulsation. His short sentences bite. Some have felt his 'pithy, excessively sharpened style that owes much to Nietzsche and still more to Karl Kraus'[20] to be a sort of onerous mental sport: hectoring, taut, muscle-bound. Others, who feel with their ears, may hear in his words the music of damaged times, hammered out. For indeed music was his greatest love and temptation: he was a prisoner of form, half-trapped by his tremendously developed linguistic skills in wringing a multitude of variations, in a kind of circling insistence, around a theme. And the opposite is also true. This semi-imprisonment gave him a kind of access to the complicities of language. In spite of his stilted intensity, his terseness served well, and was intended to serve, a polemic end. Recognising that what Marx had viewed as ideology inhabited not only the substantive propositions of discourse but the very texture and sinew of language itself, Adorno set out to challenge and overturn, often by literary shock-tactics, both the Existentialist 'jargon of authenticity' and the journalistic habits of comfortingly facile assimilation.[21] He developed the subtleties and valencies of language against the automisms of stock response. And still, his best work was on music. Here his achievements were incomparable: roughly speaking, he did for musicology what Horowitz accomplished for the art of piano-playing. He wrote at length of Wagner, Mahler and Berg; with coruscating brilliance on Bach and Schönberg, and with elegiac tenderness on Schumann's Eichendorff-Lieder. When he talked about Beethoven, he did not sound so well.

Benjamin was a theological writer in an age of disenchantment. He was gentle, reflective, and wistfully melancholic. So much so that some people who came across him received the impression that he lived in a world of his own; although a few of his contemporaries – Adorno and Scholem, Hofmannsthal and Brecht – thought highly of him. If he did live in a world of his own, it was not a well-upholstered one. He was not exactly overburdened with common-sense, found difficulty in negotiating mundane affairs, and never had very much money. In short, he had a nose for disaster. Yet his world was neither narrow nor enclosed. It was

fertile, sunlit, and clouded. He was drawn to Brecht's capacity for
directness; received from no less a novelist than Thomas Mann the
accolade for having written an 'amazingly perspicacious and profound book' on the origins of German tragic drama, which was
actually a philosophy and history of allegory in which he detected
an elective affinity between allegorical conventions and the mood
of melancholia; reflected on the blurred focus and disturbed over-
lappings, the swiftly changing tempos and directions, the shocks
and parries of city-crossings; felt a deep affinity for Proust and
Kafka; quickly understood the hysterically murderous theatrical-
ity – what he called the 'aestheticising of politics' – of the Third
Reich; wrote poignantly of a Berlin childhood around 1900; and
pondered theological texts. Some have concluded from this that he
was eclectic; and others have even jeered with the cruelty of
incomprehension at his leaning towards both Historical
Materialism and Jewish theology. For Benjamin was seeking the
priceless. He especially loved short stories, both those which are
found in children's books and others of a more 'sophisticated'
variety; and his own writings give a slow, meditative release. Of
course they are of great density; sometimes he surpasses even
Adorno in the brevity of his formulations. But at least one source of
his distinctive discourse lay elsewhere. His chosen method was the
commentary, for which he was indebted to the profound connection in the Jewish tradition between theological argument and
language. From here radiated many of his most characteristic
stylistic devices. The open form of his commentaries sought not to
present anything settled or 'contained', but to return again and
again to a motif, prising open new aspects. This strategy of reprise
was necessary to a mode of re-presentation intent on the filling-out
of meanings. By a seemingly seamless unfolding, he did not so
much impart achieved knowledge, as rather embody those processes through which insights are worked towards. So that when
reading him one may be put in mind of someone paddling in the
shallows at the edge of a vast sea, and suddenly finding that he is
swimming in the depths. Or, in some of his subtlest commentaries,
of someone writing little love-poems in prose addressed to those
with whom he would dearly wished to have spoken. For he felt
there were moments of the past that could be kneaded back into the
present. Beyond nostalgia, he sought hope. He knew the experience of slowness, even what might be called an obstinate weight
and haul of slowness; and he meditated on the question – a ques-

tion become more urgent even in our lifetime than in his – of the ways in which, somehow, renewed access might be found to a proper slowness, to a pulse beating without haste but with a fullness of life. He knew that the world secretes a multitude of recuperative moments, masked and awaiting disclosure; that works of literature were even able to communicate more good than they themselves possessed; and that it is impossible to read the same book twice. He disclosed the sacred in the fortuitous, the written, the buried.

Even if we allow for the many specific differences between these two remarkable men, and for their sometimes acrimonious intellectual quarrels, it remains true that they had one thing in common, at least. This they shared profoundly. It was an aversion – it might even be called a visceral aversion – to the idea of a system. Nor were they alone on that score. With their anti-systematic intent, they formed part of a particular historical conjuncture. They took part in what has been called the 'exodus from philosophy' which occurred in Germany especially after the First World War, the turning away from Idealism, from the constructions and critiques of more or less sedate philosophical systems comfortably housed in a temporarily pacified and relatively liberal European society which still paid heed to individuals – a turning away, towards what, in other hands, issued variously in talk about the 'anarchy of values' or the 'crisis of historicism' or the need for 'leadership' or a new 'cultural synthesis', in Existentialism and Protestant theology. That was a world in moral vertigo. And the language-consciousness of Benjamin and Adorno may be understood, in one of its aspects, as a form of defence against a kaleidescopic context in which words like sincerity, authenticity, gratuitousness, decision – words which imply a mottled moral tone of floating and clutching and wallowing, and an almost total indifference in contrasts of value – were flowing freely from twentieth-century pens. Blood flowed freely again a little later.

If we now move forward a generation, to Germany in the sixties, we find a contrast of tone, and one registered in the work of critical theory. Together with a new readiness for public debate – Habermas is here the representative figure – critical theory has renewed its links with an older German tradition. For if Adorno inclined to the aphoristic and Benjamin to the labyrinthine, Habermas' characteristic manner is one of a sustained seriousness which is more recognisably part of the habits of German 'Geistesges-chichte', in which the elaboration of particular arguments and the 'placing' of those arguments in an unfolding history of argument are viewed as integral elements of a single enterprise. But if his manner can be situated within certain conventions, his tone is his own: systematic, responsible, considerate, courageous. The roughage of his language presses through to a virtual audience; and he does not condescend. Hence the difficulty with Habermas is perhaps most likely to be found neither in terseness nor in allusiveness but rather in a consequent tone of high seriousness. And indeed those who have a taste for philosophy and sociology seasoned with the sprightly aside, or accompanied by a more mellow urbanity, may perhaps find his prose style a trifle heavy for the most congenial digestion. But then oysters, though choice, do not give much sustenance.

Yet the modes of presentation characteristic of critical theory, although in themselves a significant constituent of that tradition, can also be a snare. Two lines of least resistance immediately offer themselves. The difficulty of the texts may provoke either dismissal or monumentalisation. Perhaps it is only too easy to mock: to hear in the tones of the Frankfurt School a note so high-pitched that it seems addressed only to a small group of the elect. Alternatively, their language might be found bewitching; and the texts may then suffer the ironical fate of feeding their own 'culture industry' – of being granted the historical respect and attention sometimes thought appropriate for museum pieces rather than provoking the sense that they speak to any needs of the present. But to treat these texts either as an 'intellectual family matter', or as historical monuments, is to refuse both the challenge of their serious intent and the difficult task of genuine criticism.

These are the problems of accessibility that need to be met at the outset. There are two distinguishable layers of resistance: the availability of the writings and the intrinsic difficulty of the texts. To become clear about this is to set in perspective a third fact: namely, that critical theory is best approached not so much as a 'branch of sociology' but rather as a phenomenon of German intellectual history, with its own culturally specific conventions of argument and inquiry. Nowhere is this more transparent than in the meanings clustered within the concept of critique itself. In a programmatic essay Horkheimer cited Marx's *Critique of Political*

Economy as the paradigm for a critical theory of society;[22] but the pre-history of Marx's own concept of critique remains of central and independent importance for the tradition. The choice of the epithet 'critical' is the token of a multiple allegiance.

The word critique, like the word crisis, is derived from the Greek 'κρίνειν'.[23] It contained a number of overlapping connotations; specifically, it referred to the activities of separating, judging, and deciding. Within the content of antique usage, the word critique referred to three particular spheres of activity. It was applied primarily in the administration of justice; Aristotle used the term 'κρίσις' to refer to a judicial decision in which order is re-established in a dispute. Subsequently, there developed a medical use of the term κρίσις; here is meant the decisive turning-point of an illness. And finally, the related term κριτικός acquired a new meaning towards the Hellenistic period; here it referred to the study of literary texts.

It was with these three background connotations – legal, medical and philological – that the term 'critique' was received, via Latin, into modern European languages during the seventeenth century, reaching German towards the end of the century through French. During the intervening period, between Antiquity and Renaissance, two strata of these inherited meanings had moved in relative separation. The word 'crisis' was applied solely in a medical context right through into the seventeenth century; whereas the term criticus/grammaticus continued to refer, as in Antiquity, to the activity of grammarians. The Renaissance witnesses the re-focusing and resumption of the term 'critic' as grammarian, or more precisely, as philologist. In this context a narrower meaning of the word critique was crystallised. Critique meant the philological criticism of literary texts. Its activity consisted in a return to an original condition, and in a determination to reconstruct the authenticity of a source. Given this meaning, the period of time which elapsed between the activity of producing the text in question and the critical activity of reading it appeared essentially as a period of time in which the purity of a source had become corrupted. Historical processes were viewed as processes of fall, of decay; and it was the aim of a critique to combat that decay. The ravages effected by historical processes were to be revoked, so far as possible, by philological critique. Philological criticism was the activity of reconstruction.[24]

In this sense, the term critique was used by Humanists and

Reformers to describe the art of informed judgement appropriate to the study of ancient texts, whether the Classics or the Bible. For a time this critical activity was a weapon in the hands of the warring religious parties. But it was a double-edged weapon. Catholics might use philological methods in seeking to demonstrate the necessity of Church tradition, and Protestants might use the same method in supporting the primacy of Scripture; but in this process the art of critique itself began to claim a status independent of both Church and Scripture. First placed at the service of the one or the other, the appeal to critique gradually displaced the criterion of truth from revelation towards clear and rational, or 'critical', thought. This ironic reversal comes clearly to light in the dispute between Simon and Capelle. In his *Histoire critique du vieux testament* of 1678 Simon's defence of Church orthodoxy by resort to textual exegesis has the effect of driving a wedge between his overt argument and its latent implications; for here the meaning attached to the term critique undergoes a shift of emphasis, so that it comes to refer to a procedure in its own right.[25]

Thus it was through the thicket of religious disputes focused on textual criticism of the Bible that a new position began to emerge. The warring churches now found themselves confronted by a common enemy. A new line of demarcation had opened up between reason and revelation, and the word critique acquired polemical overtones which it was never subsequently to lose. If any particular turning-point can be singled out, it is the publication of Bayle's *Dictionnaire historique et critique* in 1697. From then onwards the concepts of 'reason' and 'critique' were indivisible. Critique came to be seen no longer as a symptom of the sharpening opposition between reason and revelation. It was viewed as itself the activity which separated the two spheres. It was the essential activity of reason.

This change was given concentrated expression in Bayle's idea of a 'republic of letters': an idea which was to inform the mental world of the Enlightenment, exercised a considerable influence on Kant, and casts a refracted light much later still in the work of Habermas. Bayle's fundamental displacement of accent, from critique as *method* to critique as *principle*, meant that the activity in question extended far beyond philological criticism. When he spoke of the 'republic of letters', what he had in mind was a public arena in which a guiltless struggle of all against all held sway. 'La Critique d'un livre ne tend qu'à montrer qu'un Auteur n'a pas tel et tel degré de lumière'; and as such it made evident to the public at large 'les fautes qui sont dans un livre.'[26] To promote a republic of letters under the banner of critique was to turn the tables. Through the reaction of the Church to philological criticism of the Bible, the word 'critique' had acquired negative and destructive connotations. Bayle accepted this, and proceeded to acknowledge his faith in it: 'La raison humaine . . . est un principe de destruction, non pas d'édification.'[27] Critique is certainly committed to the task of seeking truth; but to a truth which has yet to be established. Whence it follows that critical activity does not yield truth directly, but indirectly. Truth is to be reached, in the first instance, through the destruction of appearances and illusions. This notion of a republic of letters presupposes the equality of all participants in the process of critical activity. And that, in turn, rests on a further premise. It is now assumed that truth flourishes, not through the illumination of human understanding by inherited traditions, but rather through the medium of a communicative struggle. An important corollary flows from this premise. The model now adopted by enlightened critique forbids action informed by any political theory which follows, consciously and explicitly, from the conviction of the truth of its own theory. On the contrary: it is here assumed that the cause of truth will be advanced independently of the intentions of separate individuals, through the work of free communication. It is a cause which will be advanced only on condition that critical activity becomes a motive force for the systematic correction of error.

For a time those who engaged in this activity refrained from impinging upon the political competence of the state. Once again Bayle was the great exemplar. He explicitly drew a line beyond which the work of criticism could not pass: a taboo was to protect the authority of the absolutist state.[28] In 1697 this self-denying ordinance was understandable; for the horrors of civil and international wars were still present in the memory, and it was the absolutist state, with its strict separation of politics and morality, that had brought the confessional civil wars of the sixteenth and seventeenth centuries to a close. But half a century later Voltaire was still following Bayle's strategy. He too distinguished between critique on the one hand, and libels and satires on the other – a distinction intended to protect his critiques from the charge of political intent.[29] Yet eventually, as before, the peaceful co-existence of competences began to break down. That this took place in the mid eighteenth century is no accident: it occurred at precisely the point when the critique of revelation appeared to have been secured. From Bayle to Voltaire, from Voltaire to Diderot, the writings of the critics became gradually politicised. Ostensibly confined to the 'République des lettres', the activity of critique became first indirectly, and later directly, political. In salons, clubs, lodges and coffee-houses a new moral authority – the 'public' – found its earliest institutions.[30] Critique became one of its slogans and an endless stream of books and essays included the word 'critique' and 'critical' in their title. Voltaire proclaimed critique the Tenth Muse; Diderot asserted that everything was submitted to its law, and Kant could rightly claim in the 1781 Preface to his *Critique of Pure Reason* that his age was the true age of critique and that neither religion nor the legislature were exempt from its test. The process of critique had acquired public force.

But precisely what kind and degree of public force? On this question the critics of the Enlightenment equivocated. Sometimes they affirmed the public implications of their criticism as provocatively as possible; at other times they were more coy. The *Encyclopédie* states that the critic is a reader who knows how to distinguish – how to separate the truth from the false, virtue from fame, good from bad taste, and so on. Yet all these distinctions skirt around the political problem which they implicitly contain. And the mixed messages continue. In the *Encyclopédie* of 1779 the article on 'Critics' refuses to admit that their writings have political implications; yet in the article on 'Critique' in the same year we find the assertion that 'Il est du moins incontestable qu'elle décide des actions publiques'.[31] The same equivocation reappears when we observe Turgot advising the King of France on the problem of religious toleration. He speaks with two voices. At one moment he is talking in political categories and addressing the King; at the next he is talking in moral categories and addressing the human being.[32] In 1784 Schiller spells out the same dualism in the sphere of aesthetics: the theatre, he explains, plays the role of an immunised political critique. Here it is the separated space between the world of theatrical spectacle and the world of social reality that reproduces the conceptual dualism of morality and politics.[33] And the philosophy of history is infected by this too. The critics identify their indirect political plans with the immanent course of history, thus blurring the fact that a direct onslaught on the machinery of the state might actually take place; in this variation on the theme, the tension between the critical public and the absolutist state can be displaced on to the future. So it comes as no surprise that whether we turn to Voltaire or to Diderot, to Condorcet or to Wieland, we are unable to find an idea of revolution which is, strictly speaking, a political concept. For none of these writers think in terms of a political opposition between state authority and civil war. What they always have in mind is a moral antithesis between slavery and revolution.[34]

These equivocations – they might also be called a systematic network of hypocrisy – were strategies of defence. The distinction between morals and politics looked two ways: it offered a means of removing the political basis from beneath the absolutist state, while at the same time obscuring the fact that this was taking place. The strategy exacted a price. It meant that the public dimension of critique remained blunted. Until the outbreak of revolution in 1789 the political awareness of the intelligentsia – their sense of what a revolution, a civil war, would mean in practice – continued to be blurred by the overriding conceptual distinction between morals and politics.

This distinction has a post-history which stretches long beyond 1789. The continuing allegiance of critical theory to the Enlightenment, which gives rise to a nostalgia manifest in works as different as Horkheimer's *Eclipse of Reason* and Habermas' *Strukturwandel der Öffentlichkeit*, indicates a commitment to this Enlightenment understanding of critique.

But critical theory is indebted in particular to two new meanings of critique, in which the heritage of the Enlightenment has been once more assimilated and reformulated. These have their origin in German Idealist philosophy. It is important to distinguish between these two new senses, one originating in Kant, the other in Hegel.

The model of critique characteristic of the Enlightenment undergoes in Kant a basic structural change. For the thinkers of the Enlightenment the notion of a 'republic of letters' was a central, organising image; critical activity was seen, characteristically, as an external discussion with a partner. Kant subjected this position to a double attack. He demonstrated that, in principle, both of the contending partners in any such discussion possessed reason, and, equally, that both made false use of it. This demonstration made possible a new concept of critique. An inter-subjective conception is now superseded by an inner-subjective one. But if the activity of critique is, in this sense, internalised, then it follows that it must turn against itself. Whence the famous ambiguity in the title of Kant's work: the *Critique of Pure Reason*. Here Reason is viewed as at once the subject and the object of critique. This is Kant's contribution to the Enlightenment. It is not so much a break, as rather the point at which Kant assimilates the Enlightenment by going beyond it. In agreement with the Enlightenment, he holds that the activity of critique turns against accepted authorities. But in opposition to the Enlightenment, he shows that there are more authorities susceptible to this critique than its optimism had led it to suppose; and indeed that the authorities now in question were precisely those which had previously provided the base, the point of departure, for the activity of critique. It is in this sense that we may speak of Kant's critique as the self-critique of the Enlightenment.[35]

Critique, in this Kantian sense, denoted reflection on the *conditions* of possible knowledge: on the potential capacities of human beings possessing the faculties of knowing, speaking and acting. In the *Critique of Pure Reason* Kant set out to answer the questions: what are the conditions of our knowledge through which modern natural science is possible and how far does this knowledge extend? He wished to locate the range of inevitable 'subjective' conditions which both make any theory in natural science possible and place limits upon that theory.

Kant saw that our understanding confronted a difficulty similar to that faced by any producer who seeks to impose a particular form on unyielding matter. The *Critique* begins from the fact that only an incoherent profusion of impressions or sensations are given in perception. Since, on the other hand, we always perceive the world as a world of ordered things, it must be our faculty of perception itself which produces order out of the variety of impressions. This is the decisive work of perception: the production of possible objects of knowledge out of the given material of impressions. The faculty of perception produces, not indeed reality itself, but the mode in which reality appears to us. Things are 'constituted' by us in the sense that we can know them only through certain a priori forms or 'categories' which are embedded in the human subject.

In this century an intensified concern with language has led to a reframing of Kant's model. Students of language now attempt to grasp the generative nature of linguistic rules in themselves; here the mastery of the rules – the emergence of a competent human subject who is able to operate the rules – becomes a secondary issue. Wittgenstein's analysis of the notion of 'following a rule'; Chomsky's concepts of 'generative rules' and 'linguistic' competence'; Lévi-Strauss' 'Kantianism without a transcendental subject' – all these have contributed to this development: namely, the rational reconstruction of the conditions which make language, cognition and action possible.

But the notion of critique contains a second new meaning, whose origin is to be found in Hegel. To say this is in a sense to make a paradoxical assertion. Anyone who searches for the word 'critique' in Hegel's systematic major works will at first be disappointed; for the most part it is absent. Yet the inquiry can proceed as soon as the distinction between word and concept is acknowledged. Even if we assume that a conceptual structure may be incomplete, we cannot conclude that a particular conceptual structure has a gap in it simply from the fact that a specific word, which we know to be pertinent, is missing or avoided. The 'history' of any concept – which, in principle, must remain always incomplete – is incomplete in a quite particular sense so long as we refuse to pursue the concept in question into those places where we might usually expect to find it, but where it appears only rarely in the form of a word. In short: we must not be put off the track by the absence of explicit semantic landmarks. Only by refusing this temptation can we possibly track down the traces and transformations of the concept in question. The case of Hegel supports this general principle. For here the argument receives support both from the pre-history and from the post-history of the concept. Viewed from the angle of its pre-history, we find that in Hegel other words now stand in contexts in which, when reading the thinkers of the Enlightenment, the word 'critique' was normally to be met with and so could be anticipated in accordance with cultural conventions. The very fact that 'critique' had by now penetrated the most varied spheres provided both occasion and probability for leaving aside the task of constructing its basic meanings once again in an explicit fashion; the term 'critique' can simply be applied here and there. Its post-history speaks more eloquently still in support of this hypothesis. In the writings of those who come after Hegel, not only the 'Left-Hegelians' but also the 'Right-Hegelians', and of course in Marx, the term 'critique' reappears in precisely those contexts where the analyst of the concept would note the absence of the word in Hegel. From this it is surely wise, when reading Hegel, to look for the traces and transformations of the concept of critique in other words. For what has happened is that the plenitude of meaning which the concept had already achieved before Hegel had been subjected by him to controlled assimilation. The culturally inherited meanings are re-structured by him, even while they continue to inform the expectations which the reader brings to the new, Hegelian meanings.[36]

In this sense, critique in Hegel denotes reflection on a system of *constraints* which are humanly produced: distorting pressures to which individuals, or a group of individuals, or the human race as a whole, succumb in their process of self-formation. In the *Phenomenology of Mind* Hegel developed a concept of 'reflection' which presents the idea of a liberation from coercive illusions. This notion was perhaps most vividly expressed in that section of the *Phenomenology* which treats of the relationship between Master and Slave.[37] Hegel portrays the experience of the Slave as the over-coming of a resistance. The Master–Slave relation is to be under-stood in terms of their connection with material things. At the outset the Master, having obtained possession of the Slave's labour, tries to reduce him to a mere instrument of his will, a tool which he interposes between himself and nature so that he is protected from direct encounter with the negative side of things, from those qualities in things by virtue of which they are experi-enced as sources of resistance and constraint. But it is precisely the constraint imposed by the Master on the Slave that opens up for the latter the possibility of a growth beyond the given conditions of his existence. It is true that the life of the Slave remains distorted to the extent that his aims are limited by the commands of the Master; and yet he comes to see the objects on which he works no longer simply as bundles of resistance, for by working on them he has precipitated his human capacities into them, so that, as moulded by him, they come to reflect back to him his own human-ity. His labour transforms nature, and therefore himself, for he is now faced by a world which embodies his self-assertion as a subject. Here the way in which the Slave views his situation and the way in which he acts within it belong inextricably together; a change in the Slave's 'theory' about his condition entails a change in his 'practice', in his action within the given context. And the point is a general one, since the Master–Slave relation is for Hegel an example of a universal feature of human life and thought. This feature is what he calls the 'negative'. The negative connotes those historical forces which are incompatible with a certain form of social life and which act upon it destructively: but forces which nonetheless arise inevitably out of the particular social structure which they negate and surpass. Human rationality has a history which consists in the criticism in life and in thought of the constraints imposed by each of its specific historical forms. Hence this understanding of critique implies a particular narrative structure in which the potentialities for development of a given mode of thought or a given social condition are latent within the very structure of the initial terms.

Just as in this century an intensified interest in language has led to a reformulation of Kant's model, so the concern with constraints on human action has been elaborated by psychoanalysis. Without explicitly invoking the idea of a critique, Freud proposed what was in effect a new procedure of critical reflection. The constraints which this reflection seeks to penetrate are resistant because their weight is anchored within. Freud's 'subject' suffers under the compulsive pressure of restricted patterns of behaviour and perception; he deludes himself about his own actions; he colludes, by internalisation, with the constraints that have been imposed upon him. Only by grasping these illusions can the subject, as it were, free himself from himself: he liberates himself from the internalised conflicts which blinded him in his self-awareness and lamed him in his actions. Critique is here grounded in a specific experience, which is set down in Freud's psychoanalysis, in Hegel's *Phenomenology of Mind*, and in Marx's critique of ideology: the experience of an emancipation by means of critical insight into relationships of power, the strength of which derives, at least in part, from the fact that these relationships have not been seen through.

It is perhaps helpful to refer to the first type of critique as 'reconstruction' and to the second type of critique as 'criticism'. There are at least three important differences between *reconstruction* and *criticism*.[38]

Firstly, reconstruction (as proposed for instance by Kant or Chomsky) tries to understand anonymous systems of rules which can be followed by any subject, provided he has the requisite competences. Criticism (as proposed for instance by Hegel or Freud) is brought to bear on something not anonymous but particular; it examines the shaping of an individual's identity or the identity of a group. Hence it entails the explicit reference to a subject.

Secondly, reconstruction is based on data which are considered to be objective, like sentences, actions, or cognitive insights; these are the conscious operations of the human actor. Criticism, in contrast, is brought to bear on objects of experience whose 'objectivity' is called into question; criticism supposes that there is a degree of inbuilt deformity which masquerades as the reality and it seeks to remove this distortion and thereby to make possible the liberation of what has been distorted. Hence it entails a conception of emancipation.

Thirdly, reconstruction explains what is considered to be 'correct' knowledge; for instance the knowledge we must acquire if we are to operate rules competently. Criticism, however, aims at changing or even removing the conditions of what is considered to be a false or distorted consciousness. Thus reconstruction, by explaining rules which we follow implicitly, may lead to a broadening of the range and a greater sophistication in the possession of our theoretical knowledge. It may do this without necessarily changing our practical conduct. Criticism, on the other hand, renders transparent what had previously been hidden, and in doing so it initiates a process of self-reflection, in individuals or in groups, designed to achieve a liberation from the domination of past constraints. Here a change in practice is therefore a constitutive element of a change in theory.

In addition to assimilating the Enlightenment understanding of critique as oppositional thinking, the main exponents of critical theory have used the idea of critique in both of these new senses – without always making the fact of this new double usage sufficiently clear. They have employed the term to denote reflection on the conditions of possible knowledge; and they have also used it to denote the analysis of constraints to which classes of individuals are subject. The Enlightenment, Kant, and Hegel: these, then, are the three strata in the pre-history of critique.

2

Horkheimer's critical theory

Horkheimer mapped out his project for a critical theory of society in a series of programmatic essays written between 1931 and 1937;[1] from these the elements of his initial position may be distilled. Its starting-point, most succinctly presented in his 'Notes on Science and Crisis' of 1932, is the connection between contemporary developments in science and society.[2] He distinguishes two levels of crisis.

The first level he calls economic. He sees an evident conflict in the fact that, although social wealth is immensely greater than in all previous eras, society in its present form is unable to make effective use of the powers it has developed and the wealth it has amassed. 'The economy is in large measure dominated by monopolies, and yet on the world scale it is disorganised and chaotic.'[3] So society finds itself in the throes of a crisis which seems to demonstrate the impotence of liberal democracy and the self-destructive tendency inherent in capitalism.

The second level he calls scientific. By 'science' he means what outside the German language-area are generally referred to as the natural sciences and the human sciences. Science, in Horkheimer's view, shares the fate of the other productive forces; its 'application is sharply disproportionate' to its 'high level of development and to the real needs of mankind'.[4] Specifically, science is concerned with comprehensive relationships; yet 'it has no realistic grasp of that comprehensive relationship upon which its own existence and the direction of its work depend, namely society'.[5] There is a discrepancy between, at one level, the drift towards economic crisis, and, at another level, the inability of science to meet that crisis by developing any rationally grounded system of values or any systematic analysis in the light of which that crisis might be comprehended.

This discrepancy, Horkheimer believes, is not fortuitous. The problems of science are said to 'mirror' those of the economy. It would be wrong to infer from this image that the two crises are to be viewed as if they simply ran a parallel course. Horkheimer is unequivocal in assigning causal priority to the economic crisis. Science 'is determined in the scope and direction of its work not by its own tendencies alone, but, in the last analysis, by the necessities of social life itself'.[6] Hence the root of deficiencies in the scientific enterprise must be found 'not in science itself but in the social conditions which hinder its development'.[7] An understanding of the crisis of science depends on a correct theory of the present 'social life-process in its totality': 'in so far as we can speak of a crisis in science, this crisis is inseparable from the general crisis'.[8]

It is important at this point to note a discrepancy in Hork-heimer's analysis. The discrepancy is between the statement of his diagnosis and the more detailed process of its elaboration: the difference between his 'Notes on Science and Crisis' and his other programmatic essays marks the point of this fissure. It is true that, in the 1932 essay and elsewhere, he explicitly assigns causal pri-macy to the economic crisis; but, surveying the essays written between 1931 and 1937 as a whole, it is evident that the substance of his analysis focuses almost exclusively on the scientific crisis. How significant or insignificant this displacement of accent really is must remain for the moment an open question. What requires investigation, in the first instance, is the area on which his essays concentrate.

Horkheimer advances his arguments along two fronts. The first concerns the relationship between philosophy and empirical research. The second concerns the relationship between the sci-ences in general and the development of society. Horkheimer presents a critique the elaboration of which necessarily leads from the first to the second level of analysis. In each case he asks the questions: how are those relationships at present constituted, and how should they be constituted?

Let us turn to Horkheimer's first area of preoccupation. How is the relationship between philosophy and empirical research at present constituted, and how should it be constituted? Horkheimer begins by arguing that the connection between

philosophy and empirical research is characterised by the juxtaposition of two extreme positions. One pole, represented by
German Lebensphilosophie and phenomenology, sought
systematically to discredit empiricism and pragmatism. This
stream of philosophy fostered an overt hostility to science which,
reinforced by the influence of Heidegger, continued to exert after-
effects on the intellectual life of the Federal Republic. The other
pole was represented by the empirical orientation of social
research. This position, which the group around Horkheimer
encountered at first hand during their period of exile in the United
States, was prepared to concede truth-content only to the
specialised empirical disciplines as then practised and understood.
Neither of these extreme positions, according to Horkheimer, was
able to provide a firm ground for a critical theory of society: a basis,
that is, in terms of which it might be possible, at least at the level of
interpretation, to respond appropriately to the catastrophic trend
of contemporary developments. Both speculative philosophy and
empirical research averted their gaze from the oncoming catastrophe. Some concepts of a totality were to be found in current
philosophical writings, but only in such rarefied notions as 'Being',
'Existence', and 'Life', in which the material reality of the world
was transfigured into etherealised abstractions. Any explicit concept of a totality was absent from empirical research, which overtly
dismissed such a concept from its range of reference. Abstract
empiricisms and abstract totalities complemented each other as
concave to convex. Both fell short of the necessary task: 'Science
has to do with a knowledge of comprehensive relationships; yet it
has no realistic grasp of that comprehensive relationship upon
which its own existence and the direction of its work depend,
namely, society.'[9]

Ignoring – or overriding – the seeming disjunction between
philosophical speculation and empirical research, Horkheimer
proposed a fertilising interpretation of 'theoretical' and 'empirical'
work. A form of social philosophy was required which would
counteract the splintering development of separate empirical sciences by assimilating their results while setting them in a new
analytical framework. It must exercise directive control in its
selection of problem-areas, and integrative pressure in reworking
the results of specialised investigations. To this end, it did of
course need to process data provided by empirical research; but
this it sought to restructure in accordance with its own procedure.

Horkheimer described this critical activity by distinguishing
between two processes. These he called 'Forschung' and 'Darstellung'.[10] 'Forschung' referred to the research carried out by particular empirical investigations. 'Darstellung' referred to the activity
by which the results of such investigations, in a kind of rotatory
movement, were informed both by an anticipating comprehension
and a subsequent representation. The work of research – 'Forschung' – which assimilates material by analytical decomposition,
must be guided by the work of representation – 'Darstellung' –
which recomposes the appropriate material into new conceptual
frameworks. As Horkheimer saw the matter, this proposal entailed
the rejection of traditional logical procedures. In traditional logic,
in his view, a change in concepts was conceived as a process in
which the original classes within a system of classification were
made more specific by the provision of new subspecies. To put the
point perhaps over-sharply: all changes entailed the addition of
subspecies to previously existing categories. In all change, embodi-
ments or emanations of fixed ideas and essences are reached by
new specifications and examples. This meant, in effect, that
change affected only the 'lower', more deficient levels of being.
Horkheimer's critical method, as he understood it, was conceived
in opposition to this. It was a theoretical activity in which empirical research provided the elements for a reconstruction: a reconstruction in which these elements could no longer remain what
they were. A critical attack subjected them to a reconstruction
within which they were assimilated into a new conceptual structure. Marx's *Capital* provided an imposing instance of this procedure.[11] Marx assimilated into his work many of the concepts of
economic analysis as it existed in his time: exchange-value, price,
labour-time, and so on. Yet in the process of his representations the
old categories received new significance. They were made to contribute to a new construct whose *raison d'être* contradicted their
static observations and their isolated applications. Marx's critical
method in its entirety opposed the system of classical economics:
opposing it, nonetheless, by transferring the particular concepts of
his antagonists into his own conceptual structure. The antagonists'
concepts were taken over and in this way surpassed. This, as
Horkheimer saw it, was a method of total reconstruction. No
partial aspect of social life and no isolated phenomenon may be
comprehended without relating it to the conceptual whole, the
social structure of production in its entirety. This notion of

totality does not refer to a metaphysical substratum of being. It refers rather to a structural level of analysis within whose framework the results of 'empirical' research are reconstituted.

This striving for a concept of totality based on the distinction between 'Forschung' and 'Darstellung' was brought to practical fruition by the organisational structure which fostered critical theory – the Institute for Social Research.[12] Borrowing a couple of terms from mainstream sociology, it could be said that 'Forschung' and 'Darstellung' were functions which defined different roles. The role of 'Darstellung' entailed a number of functions. Their performance involved the selection of problems for investigation; the differentiation, with the aid of empirical control, of the way in which such problems had initially been posed; and the formulation of results both within the Institute and to the world at large. The role of 'Forschung' likewise entailed a number of functions. Their performance involved the provision of empirical data for the interpretation of set questions; the exercise of control over the process of representation; and the suggestion of ways in which the results of research might be translated into practice. This distinction between 'Darstellung' and 'Forschung' yielded a fertile basis for a differentiation of roles within the organisational structure of the Institute. Horkheimer undertook the role of 'Darstellung', while his colleagues worked on specific areas. Pollock was a political economist, Fromm a psychoanalyst, Löwenthal a literary critic, Marcuse a specialist in the history of philosophy, and Adorno a student of musicology. Among this group of many talents, Adorno's were evidently the most wide-ranging. Versed not only in musicology, but in philosophy, literary criticism, psychoanalysis and sociology, he was the interdisciplinary person par excellence. All the more telling, then, is the fact that, apart from a few essays in the later issues of the *Zeitschrift*, his contributions were at first confined to musicology. The exception proved the rule. The distinction between 'Forschung' and 'Darstellung' was anchored in the institutional structure of the Institute for Social Research.

Let us now turn to consider Horkheimer's second area of preoccupation: how is the relationship between science and society at present constituted, and how should it be constituted?

Just as he argues that the relation between philosophy and empirical research is marked by the juxtaposition of two extreme positions, so he argues that the connection between science and society is determined by a double abstraction. Theory as traditionally understood regards the practical context within which it inevitably takes place as external to the procedures of theoretical activity itself. The fact that theory is in some sense connected with practice is not denied; but the connection is viewed as an accidental, not an intrinsic, element in the constitution of theory. 'The social genesis of problems, the real situations in which science is put to use, and the purposes which it is made to serve are all regarded by science as external to itself.'[13] This self-interpretation of theory entails a second level of abstraction: abstraction from historical practice is duplicated by internalisation. The individual who is a theorist is himself split in two. 'The scholarly specialist "as scientist" regards social reality and its products as extrinsic to him, and "as citizen" exercises his interest in them through political articles, membership in political parties or social organisations, and participation in elections. But he does not unify these two activities, and his other activities as well, except, at best, by psychological interpretation.'[14] Whence there arises a double abstraction, at once 'external' and 'internal', of scientific theory from the material context within which it is contained – the process of production. Theory is therefore ideological.

It is ideological because it fails to recognise the precondition of its own existence. Here Horkheimer assumes Marx's premise. The process of labour 'is the general condition for the metabolism between men and nature; it is the everlasting nature-imposed condition of human existence and therefore is independent of every social form of that existence or rather, is common to every such form'.[15] The 'metabolism' between man and nature is independent of specific historical structures. Horkheimer reaffirms that all branches of production are 'particular instances of the way in which society comes to grips with nature'.[16] The sciences are one component among many. As 'one of man's productive powers', they remain 'moments in the social process of production, even if they are almost or entirely unproductive in the narrower sense'.[17] In Horkheimer's view this point holds in principle, even when the sciences do not further the interests of any important sector of society and are not in any obvious way productive in the sense of forming part of a money-making enterprise. But if science is part of the whole labour process, the metabolism between man and nature, it is also of course historically variable. Agrarian and industrial productive structures take effect within a specific division of labour, as that is organised at any particular stage of development. Science is no exception. The scholar's activities take place alongside all other socially structured activities. The absence of evident connections between his own activities and those going on around him causes the social function of the sciences, as they are constituted by any specific productive process, to remain opaque to their own practitioners. Yet if the essential activities of the theorist remain opaque even to himself, that merely reproduces the condition common to all branches of production. Contemporary society has a two-sided character. It is the 'product of work as well as the organisation which mankind was capable of and has provided for itself in the present era', yet its structures are 'comparable to nonhuman natural processes' because they are 'not the creations of a unified, self conscious will'.[18] Any attempt at self-interpretation is impeded by this constraint; and thus scientists cannot understand the productive process within which their activities as scientists are embedded. Whence there arises a homology between the – false – capitalist concept of a contractually 'free' economic subject, and the – equally false – scientific concept of a 'value-free' theoretical procedure. 'The seeming self-sufficiency enjoyed by the work-process whose course is supposedly determined by the very nature of the object corresponds to the seeming freedom of the economic subject in bourgeois society. The latter believe they are acting according to personal determinations, whereas even in their most complicated calculations they but exemplify the working of an incalculable social mechanism.'[19]

Critical theory aims to comprehend this condition in order to make objectively possible emancipation from it. Its end is the abolition in thought and in reality of the opposition, not only between philosophy and empiricism, but, at a deeper level that determines this opposition, between science as 'abstract theory' and science as 'theoretical practice'. It seeks to surpass the opposition within each theoretician himself between the 'scientist' and the 'citizen'. The critical theorist 'has a concept of man as in conflict with himself until this opposition is removed'.[20] This conflict cannot be surpassed by particular practical reform within the given structure of society; piecemeal social engineering is fore-doomed to miss the mark. The aim of critical activity cannot be the elimination of particular abuses, for such abuses must be understood as connected necessarily and systematically with the way in which the whole social structure is organised. The goal of critique cannot therefore be the better 'functioning' of any component within the structure; the critical theorist looks instead towards a wholly 'new kind of organisation of work'.[21] To the extent to which he sees the objects which he studies as 'products which in principle should be under human control and, in the future at least, will in fact come under it, these realities lose the character of pure facticity'.[22] This interest in 'emancipation' is decisive. The critical theorist does nor simply regard social structures as products of human activity, nor simply condemn the absence of rational control. It is insufficient to pass judgement on a prevailing structure that is, as an evaluation, both sweeping and negative. The process of judgement must establish the vital link with a material force capable of transforming the given constraints. The critical theorist must establish 'a dynamic unity with the oppressed class', so that his analysis of present conditions is 'not merely an expression of the concrete historical situation but also a force within it to stimulate change'.[23] He can establish this 'dynamic unity' only by forgoing illusions about it. He must acknowledge that 'even the situation of the proletariat is, in this society, no guarantee of correct knowledge';[24] and that if he were merely to restrict himself to formulating the feelings and ideas of the proletariat he would be practising a form of social psychology, not going beyond it. If he evades the effort of establishing temporary opposition to the proletariat he 'only makes the masses blinder and weaker than they need be',[25] and so ends by colluding with the capitalist exploitation of the proletariat. If he is to realise his goal of being a 'promoting factor in the development of the masses',[26] the critical theorist must explicitly sharpen the conflict 'between the advanced sectors of the class and the individuals who speak out the truth concerning it';[27] the possibility of tension between the theoretician and the class which his thinking is to serve is always present. There precisely resides the dynamic unity he seeks: the unity of the social forces which promise liberation is at the same time their distinction. The practice of critique must be turned 'not only against the conscious defenders of the status quo but also against distracting, conformist, or utopian tendencies within his own household'.[28] Household tensions can only be reduced by recognition. That is what Horkheimer means when he says that the profession of the critical theorist 'is the struggle of which his own thinking is a part and not something self-sufficient and separable from the struggle'.[29]

Not surprisingly, Horkheimer eventually cites Marx's *Critique of Political Economy* as the paradigm for a critical theory of society.[30] It is assigned this position by virtue of strengths which are considered to be both formal and substantive. Formally, Horkheimer claims commitment to Marx's critique as signalling that point in the history of the human species where accounts are definitely settled with bourgeois philosophy and its attempt to comprehend reality systematically; its real aspiration is assimilated while its metaphysical pretension is abandoned. Marx is viewed as the thinker who demonstrated the possibility of interpreting the history of the human species through an analysis focused on the most advanced social formation, the capitalist mode of production. This made available a powerful conceptual apparatus which required neither metaphysical principles nor empirical naïveté. Substantively, Horkheimer claims commitment to Marx's theory of capitalism. In following his example, critical theory begins 'with the idea of the simple exchange of commodities', and proceeds to show 'how an exchange economy ... must necessarily lead to a heightening of those social tensions which in the present historical era lead in turn to wars and revolution'.[31] According to this argument, Marx's analysis, far from being an analytical reconstruction applicable only to characteristically nineteenth-century conditions, continues to provide a firm ground-plan for the interpretation of the present age. With the aid of the concepts provided by Marx's theory of capitalism, it becomes possible to comprehend the epoch-making changes of contemporary history – the concentration of capital, the spread of imperialism, and the recurrence of economic crises.[32]

It would be idle to suppose that Marx's bequest provides a point of rest. No doubt it might be tempting to regard it as a universal schema which designates an inexorable determinism steering the course of future events, rather than as a framework within which to focus new investigations. But anyone who yields to this temptation succeeds only in transforming back Marx's gift into a closed system of dogmatic metaphysics. They then fall back behind what Marx had achieved in his own *Critique*. To combat such regressive possibilities, Horkheimer proposes that new areas of investigation be opened up by critical theory. He singles out two aspects of social life the investigation of which should supplement the critique of political economy: the psychological disposition characteristic of different social groups and the theory of culture.

Does this exhaust the premises which underlie Horkheimer's project? In other words, how seriously does he really intend us to take the claim that critical theory finds its paradigm in Marx's *Critique of Political Economy*? Three considerations prompt serious doubts.

First of all, there is a remarkable elusiveness about the way in which Marx is cited as the author of canonical texts. Precisely at that point in his programmatic statement of 1937 when Horkheimer introduces the term 'critical activity', a note of embarrassment is audible. In employing the word critique, he explains, we must understand that 'the term is used here less in the sense it has in the idealist critique of pure reason than in the sense it has in the dialectical critique of political economy'.[33] This remark, located at the strategic point of transition in his exposition of the differences between traditional and critical theory, strikes a discord between the title and the text of his essay. The discord has been struck by a double suppression. Horkheimer's explanation is couched in the form of a hedgingly comparative statement: the term critical should be understood 'less in the sense' of the idealist 'than' in the sense of the materialist dialectic. And, more significantly, the explanation is demoted out of the main body of the text into a footnote. This double suppression prompts suspicion. For it is no isolated semantic slip. As Director of the Institute for Social Research, Horkheimer must be held responsible for a series of textual modifications to which some of Benjamin's work was subjected before it was printed in the *Zeitschift für Sozialforschung*. Most notably, the version of his essay on 'The Work of Art in the Age of Mechanical Reproduction' which appeared in 1936 was altered by such substitutions as 'totalitarian doctrine' for 'fascism', 'constructive forces of mankind' for 'communism', and 'modern warfare' for 'imperialist warfare'; and Benjamin's preface, which directly referred to Marx, was entirely omitted. Doubts burgeon further still when one turns back to the inaugural address given by Horkheimer in 1931 on 'The Current Condition of Social Philosophy and the Task of an Institute of Social Research'. On close scrutiny this turns out to contain a number of directives and statements of intent which are notable mainly for being tantalisingly unspecific. Thus we are told at one point that Hegelian Idealism in its essential features already merits the claim to be called a social philosophy because it interprets the basic conditions of the individual's life as manifest not in his personal actions but in the 'life of the whole' to which he belongs;[34] at another point, the goal of social philosophy is said to be an interpretation of the fate of men 'insofar as they are not merely individuals but members of a community';[35] and at yet another point the aim of the Institute's research is described as an attempt to construct a 'theory of the historical course of the contemporary epoch'.[36] At no point is Marx mentioned by name; nor is the theoretical object of *Capital*, the capitalist mode of production in general, referred to directly. What we are offered instead is a diffuse bundle of terms – 'society', 'community', 'epoch'. At each twist of the argument the object which supposedly provides the unity of the proposed intellectual exercise shifts. What these terms – society, community, epoch – have in common only serves to reinforce suspicion: all of them are derived from conventions of German historical and social inquiry which had either continued to develop in virtual ignorance of Marx's work, or had been deliberately elaborated in explicit opposition to it. For all these semantic shifts it is of course possible to provide specific, local justifications: the necessity to keep a carefully guarded profile amid the turbulence of the collapsing Weimar Republic; the advisability of making tactical adaptations to the counter-revolutionary climate of the United States in which the Institute had recently found a point of rest; the confusions, uncertainties and reticences inevitably associated with preliminary statements of a large-scale research programme. Yet the fact remains that the semantic shifts all point away from one direction: away, that is, from an explicit and sharply focused commitment to Marx's *Critique of Political Economy* as a paradigm.

 The point is reinforced by a second consideration. This concerns the substantive research generated by the project of a critical theory. When a project refers back to Marx's critique as providing the point of orientation for its future work the expectation is aroused that an attempt will be made to produce for the present age a critique of political economy as comprehensive as that which Marx produced for his own time. In material ways the main exponents of critical theory fail to fulfil any such expectations. They never established explicit, firm and enduring links with the already existing corpus of political thought and economic analysis instigated by Marx. Yet there was much on which they could have built. After the deaths of Marx and Engels the emergence of working class parties in Central Europe and the eruption of popular rebellions in Eastern Europe had created the preconditions for a new kind of Marxist political theory. Lenin responded by constructing a theory of class conflict in terms of political organisation and tactics, spelling out the concepts and methods necessary for a successful working class struggle in Russia; while Korsch, Lukács and Gramsci, all of whom participated directly in the revolutionary struggles in their respective countries, left behind a substantial body of political theory and strategic instruction. The same period witnessed a florescence of Marxist economic analysis. In the third volume of *Capital* Marx had enumerated a number of problems which would have to be tackled by anyone who took up his work where he was forced to leave off. Specifically, he singled out the investigation of the world market, the problem of recurrent economic crises, and the movement of market prices. After his death the transformation of the capitalist mode of production that generated monopolisation and imperialism required detailed economic analysis; and again a number of Marxist thinkers responded to the challenge. Kautsky investigated the changes in European and American agriculture; Luxemburg demonstrated the structural importance for the capitalist system of military–imperial expansion by the metropolitan powers in the Balkans, Asia and Africa; and Hilferding produced a large-scale reworking of Marxist economics to survey the capitalist mode of production on a global scale. The main exponents of critical theory failed to assimilate either the political or the economic wing of classical Marxism in such a way as to make it possible for them to elaborate this work further by any independent research of their own. This failure to assimilate a theoretical inheritance seriously impeded their ability to respond to the problems presented by the emerging political and economic landscape of the next generation. The period following the Second World War saw the establishment, for the first time in the history of bourgeois rule, of representative democracy based on universal suffrage as the normal and relatively stable structure of the state in all the main capitalist countries – the USA, Japan, West Germany, France and England. But the bourgeois-democratic state as such was never the object of any major work by the main exponents of critical theory. At the same time, the long post-war economic boom was greater than that of any earlier period in the history of capitalism; the dynamism of imperialist expansion in both the Atlantic and Pacific areas seemingly confounded classical predictions of the impending decline or crisis of capitalism and presented Marxist economists with a whole set of new problems. Here again the chief representatives of critical theory produced no work of major importance.

It might be argued in their defence that in this the work of critical theory is a specific example of the general failure of self-styled Marxists to produce a critique of political economy throughout the whole period from the collapse of European revolutions at the end of the First World War to the emergent global crises of the early seventies.[37] But the persuasiveness of this line of defence is blunted by a further doubt. For there is yet a third consideration which casts doubt on the explicitness of Horkheimer's intentions when he refers to the *Critique of Political Economy* as the model for a new critical theory. This concerns his historicist understanding of critical theory. When Horkheimer sees *Capital* as the model for social theory he gives as his reason the fact that in Marx's analysis 'knowledge of the historical course of society as a whole supplies the dynamic motif'.[38] Since critical theory aims to emulate this by understanding society as a whole, it must include itself in the object of its investigation; for the theoretical activity of men, no less than their practical activity, is 'a product of ever changing reality'.[39] Because critical theory has 'a historically changing object' its own procedure consists in 'the continuous alteration of the theoretician's existential judgement on society'.[40] This continuous change of social conditions, due immediately to economic developments, affects 'the way in which the culture depends on the economy, and, thus, the key ideas in the whole conception of critical theory'.[41] It follows from this that the influence of social development on the structure of the theory is 'part of the theory's doctrinal content'.[42] And since critical theory is 'a unified whole' which has its proper meaning 'only in relation to the contemporary situation', it must be admitted that 'the theory as a whole is caught up in an evolution' and that 'even the apparently more remote concepts of the theory are drawn into the evolution'.[43] The 'whole conceptual structure' of critical theory, therefore, makes 'demands for adaptation to ever new situations'.[44] And yet Horkheimer wants to insist, at the same time, that there can be no radical change in the substantive content of critical theory. 'Critical theory does not have one doctrinal substance today, another tomorrow.'[45] Its stability derives from the fact that 'the basic economic structure, the class relationship',[46] remains identical. The decisive components of the theory are conditioned by these unchanging factors and they themselves therefore cannot change until there has been a historical transformation of society. So the evolution in which the theory is caught up as a whole leaves an ineradicable core untouched; it 'does not change the theory's foundations'.[47] From this double insistence it appears that critical theory has some components which are changeable and others which are unchangeable. But then the question arises: by what criterion is it possible to distinguish the essential from the inessential constituents of the theory? By what measure, for instance, is it possible to determine whether the society of National Socialist Germany during the thirties or the society of the constitutionally democratic USA of the sixties have 'essentially' the same structure as that of England in the mid nineteenth century? The 'basic economic structure' which is appealed to, in the programmatic statement, as the ground for the unchanging substance of the theory, is never the object of a sophisticated and detailed inquiry by those whose work is supposedly justified by that programmatic statement. Presumably any differentiated study of that basic economic structure, understood in Marxist categories, would have to proceed by showing how specifically the labour theory of value could be applied in explaining the operation of that economic structure under contemporary conditions. But although the main exponents of critical theory continued to cite the categories of the labour theory of value, they did not subject those categories to sustained explanation as economic categories, and they sometimes failed even to name them explicitly. Thus it becomes difficult to avoid the growing suspicion that by constantly drawing attention to its own historicity, critical theory is loosening rather than reinforcing its links with Marx's materialist critique. Its search for a secure ground now appears to swing between the unstable poles of an absence and an affirmation: the absence of substantive work on political economy has its counterpart in the affirmation of historicity as a formal principle.

These considerations – Horkheimer's historicist account of critical theory, the absence of any substantial body of work on political economy, and the elusiveness with which Marx is cited as the instigator of social philosophy – suggest that the positions advanced by the main proponents of critical theory are best approached negatively, by locating the areas in which they diverge from their ostensible paradigm. The subsequent divergences were fourfold. From the outset there is a switch from the substructure to the superstructure. This leads to a new view of the substructure itself, as the critique of political economy is replaced by the critique of instrumental rationality. The reductionism entailed by this step prompts the emancipatory interest of critical theory to re-interpret the system of needs by assimilating, and in the process revising, Freud's metapsychology. And the continuing reduction of the political component of critical theory entailed by this step leads finally to an attempt to resuscitate the political dimension, and incorporate it as an intrinsic element of critical theory, by drawing on the tradition of hermeneutics. These four basic modifications of Marx's critique do not represent a series of co-existent possibilities; they mark rather the immanent development of a line of inquiry over the period of two generations. There is nonetheless a considerable chronological overlap between the 'stages' of this trajectory.

3

The critique of ideology

In the first phase of its movement, critical theory addressed itself to an area of inquiry referred to in Marxist theory as the superstructure. It sought to confront a complex of problems whose urgency became evident only in the wake of the First World War, but whose origins are traceable to the set of concepts provided by Marx. The difficulty they saw may be approached at the juncture where two angles intersect: the theory of ideology, and the theory of class.

Marx's concept of ideology needs to be situated within the context of his idea of critique. The theme around which his critical activity revolves is the connection between the critique of prevailing conditions and the critique of theories which offer an account of those conditions. He sees these conditions also as constraints, and theories as the necessary reinforcement of those constraints. This position is expressed in his early essay, the *Introduction to the Critique of Hegel's Rechtsphilosophie*. His critique involves a double attack. It is directed against the existing German political constitution viewed as the consequence of German conditions; and it is directed against Hegel's *Rechtsphilosophie* viewed as the highest form in which contemporary German conditions appear consciously, in the shape of a self-interpretation. From this two-pronged attack we may infer that, in Marx's view, 'reality' includes not simply the material structuring of brute facts; 'reality' refers just as much to descriptions of reality. Books are an important part of reality. It follows that Marx can quite consistently proceed to a critique of existing reality by means of a sustained critique of texts: texts in which, he argues, present reality is made most clearly manifest. Here Marx at once inherits and surpasses the Enlightenment. Marx shares with the Enlightenment the belief that the critical process eliminates what is unclear in concepts; it removes from them the forms in which the wishes characteristic of a particular milieu have received expression; and in so doing it brings this literal meaning to clear consciousness. That is what Marx meant when he said that the world has for long possessed the dream of something, of which it needs 'only' to possess the consciousness in order to possess it in reality. But Marx surpasses the Enlightenment when he sees that critical activity must take the contents of ideology, which it subjects to attack, with true seriousness. These contents are not merely illusory, but important in themselves: as symptoms of a condition which needs precisely these illusions. Although betraying little overt preoccupation with the fact of death, and hence having little feeling for the phenomenon of religion, Marx was able, on the basis of his insight, to go beyond the Enlightenment in his critique of religion. He saw not simply the negative point that real misery comes to light in religious concepts, but the positive point that the concepts themselves explicitly point to that misery. They are not only symptomatic of it; they disclose it. If, therefore, the critic of theology were to rest content with his own demonstration that religious belief is an illusion, his position, *vis-à-vis* theology, would remain deficient. He could not possibly comprehend the object of his attack. For comprehension is an essential constituent of the critical process; it must try to explain as completely as possible why the phenomenon which it claims to be illusory continues to exist. Only by taking this route could the critic possibly reach a position where he might be able to replace the wish-contents of theology in their illusory form, by his own post-ulated 'materialisation' of those contents. Only thus could he show that these contents might be 'realised'. This is what Marx meant when he said that the poverty of religion is at one and the same time the 'expression' of real poverty and 'protest' against that poverty; and when he said that the demand to abandon the illu-sions about man's condition is the demand to abandon a condition which needs those illusions.

That, in its turn, is the reason why Marx, even in those writings generally considered as belonging to his mature period, developed his critique of the capitalist mode of production principally through a critique of theories about economic production. In this sense, Marx geared his interpretation of capitalism to the con-ditions of a liberal society: to the forms, as well as to the contents, of its ideology. His critique of classical political economy, like his critiques of theology and political thought, entailed a two-pronged

attack. Fundamentally, it was a critique of the actual political–economic relationships which he considered as arising necessarily from the capitalist mode of production and distribution. But
it was also a critique of political economy, that comprehensive
self-interpretation of capitalist society which had found its most
adequate form in the writings of Adam Smith and Ricardo. The
basic theoretical object of Marx's investigations was the capitalist
productive process. But, and Marx was insistent on this point,[1] it
was impossible to grasp this object directly. The actual system of
bourgeois economy is comprehended through, and only with the
help of, a critique of economic categories. His critique of capitalism
was thus a sustained critique of theories. By rigorously following
through the premises of bourgeois economics, he sought to disclose
the contradictions between those premises and reality; by this
method he aimed to penetrate to the objectively existing contradictions in reality itself. These two prongs of his attack are necessarily
connected. He viewed the categories employed by the bourgeois
economists as inhabiting a seemingly timeless realm cut off from
the historical movement of the productive forces: they misinterpreted the transient nature of a historically specific productive
process by ascribing to its formation the attributes of natural laws
independent of historical variability. But underlying this false
independence in theory there was the equally false, and causally
more basic, independence of productive practice. Marx saw the
distortion in the categories used to interpret the world as the
expression in theory of a real distortion in the liberal capitalist
economy itself. Because of the contradiction between social production and private appropriation, the process of material production
had acquired a pseudo-autonomy independent of human needs;
the value of the goods circulating on the market were erroneously
thought to be the properties of these things in themselves, so that
they could no longer be experienced for what they truly were – the
systematically distorted expression of social relations between
classes of producers. Marx was thus able to re-interpret the
categories used by his opponents as a key to the real conditions of
which they offered an account; he produced a critique of actual
social conditions via a critique of the categories used to explain,
and thus in effect justify, those conditions. On this view, ideological concepts themselves – labour, commodity, exchange-value
and the like – by justifying what existed in systematic, discursive
propositions, offered at the same time a point of leverage for

ideology-critique: the medium of a possible confrontation between claim and reality.

The dual aspect of Marx's critique, his attack on theoretical categories and on material constraints, has often been noted; and in directing it against Adam Smith and Ricardo he was carrying through to its logical conclusion a procedure begun in his earlier attacks on Feuerbach and on Hegel. But what is less frequently acknowledged is that this strategy itself is based on a bequest of the Enlightenment: that is on the existence of and the appeal to a critical public.[2] The public sphere, in this sense, is one in which private individuals behave neither as business associates nor as legal associates; for as business associates they are concerned with their private affairs, and as legal associates they are subject to the legislative directions of a state bureaucracy. Individual citizens act together as a 'public' body when they are unconstrained; specifically, when they have the guarantee of being able to assemble together freely, to express and publish their opinions freely, and to debate matters of general interest, particularly those concerned with the conduct of the state. One could even go so far as to say that public opinion is the opponent of the executive power; in the sense, that is, that public opinion refers to the tasks of critique, control and surveillance which the public exercise in relation to organised state authority. It is no accident that the concept of a public sphere and of public opinion first took shape during the course of the eighteenth century. It was then that a distinction was for the first time made between 'opinion' and 'public opinion'. Whereas opinions – that is to say, collective values and prejudices, elements of the cultural inheritance, practices which were taken for granted – remain unchanged as a kind of historical sediment, public opinion, on the other hand, entailed a distinctively new conception and one which could be firmly established only on condition that there existed a reasoning public. Critical public discussions which took as their theme the exercise of political authority had not always existed. In modern European history they first developed during a particular phase in the emergence of bourgeois society: at the point when the principle of publicity was used to challenge the politics of the absolute monarchs. Previously, it had been a general practice for the estates to make treaties with princes by which the authority claims of either side were from time to time delimited. But the third estate broke with this traditional method for adjusting rival claims to authority. They had to break with that method, because there was no way in which the bourgeoisie could establish their power as an estate exercising a particular authority. A separation of authorities by demarcating seigneurial rights was no longer possible on the basis of a developed commercial economy. For the ownership of capitalist property guaranteed by civil law was, strictly speaking, unpolitical; the bourgeoisie were private individuals; and as such they did not 'rule'. If they were to press their claims to power against the traditional grouping of public authorities, they could not do so by directing their claims against a particular agglomeration of authority which might be 'divided' in a new way. On the contrary, the only strategy open to them was to undercut the essential principle upon which prevailing structures of authority were based. The ideas of critique, control and surveillance which the bourgeois public opposed to the old principle of authority – that is to say the new principle of publicity – aimed at nothing less than a change in the nature of authority as such, a change which aimed to transform political authority into rational authority. It was this pressure which produced the context of criticism and counter-criticism, the systematic, discursive justification of particular social arrangements, within the ambit of which Marx's ideology-critique moved.

But what is the appropriate response if it is seen that new productive processes make it possible to impede the formation of such a critical public? The question leads back to the second of the two angles, present in Marx's work, from which the problem of the superstructure needs to be rethought: the theory of class.

It is not without irony that the manuscript of Marx's major work breaks off just as he is about to embark on a definition of class; the 52nd chapter of the third volume of *Capital* is little more than a page long. But from remarks on the theme scattered throughout his work it becomes clear that, for the most part, he uses the concept in a specific way. What constitutes a class is the common objective position in relation to the means of production in a commodity-producing society. From this it may be inferred that, if a class is to have any say over its own fate, it must become aware of its position in the productive process and must be able to act concertedly in the light of this self-knowledge. Lukács later elaborated this point at some length. By considering the way in which he did this we can begin to see some of the difficulties involved in systematic discussion of the problem in a twentieth-century context.

In *History and Class Consciousness*, Lukács argued that the capitalist productive process was the first in the course of world history to be potentially transparent to the producers themselves. This possibility had to be present if capitalism was to be surpassed as a particular form of social organisation. For to overcome capitalism a change in economic structure or in individual consciousness is insufficient; a change in shared consciousness is a necessary precondition. Following Marx, Lukács argued that only the proletariat, by collective action, was capable of overcoming the split between 'subjects' and 'objects' in the historical process, in which what are in reality the products of human intentions have come to acquire the seeming objectivity of an apparatus which appears to obey its own laws. Lukács follows Marx in believing that it is the position of the proletariat within the capitalist process of production that forces it to an awareness of its situation and of the possibilities of action open to it. The proletariat can understand their class position and real interests only if they comprehend the whole productive structure of which they form a part; self-knowledge is an indispensable condition for effective action. But Lukács saw, nonetheless, that a problem of particular complexity arises at precisely this point. Marx's concepts, which he employed to disclose the workings of a society based on commodity exchange, are not conceived descriptively but critically. As concepts they bear in themselves a particular imprint: the tension of a condition which they need to surpass. The concept of the 'character mask' is a case in point. As a critical concept, the 'character mask' is conceived by Marx, quite explicitly, in a directly anti-psychological way. It refers to the historical subjects only in so far as they are members of classes; in the society which produces commodities, persons count only as 'the personifications of economic relationships as the bearers of which they encounter one another'.[3] So when Marx speaks of the 'character mask', he is not using a descriptive concept like the modern category of role.[4] Role refers to a sector of human action that is ruled by norms. But the character mask is a metaphor for the individual as a member of a class and it therefore structures his whole existence, not simply a sector of his existence. If the character mask is a critical concept in this sense, it must hold for the members of any class and not only for the capitalists. This, however, requires that the critical theorist take particular care when the activity of the oppressed class comes under discussion. In order to help the historical subjects, who can appear to others and even to themselves only as functions in the process of commodity production, to attain in reality that capacity of agency, of autonomy, which bourgeois political and social thought imputes to them as already given, this bourgeois notion of the 'subject' – whose history stretches from Descartes to the early Sartre – must first of all be unmasked. That is of course a necessary step in the Marxist critique of ideology. But there lurks a danger in this anti-psychological critique: the danger of making the 'psychological', or whatever is subsumed under that category, quite simply historically irrelevant. The 'subjective', the sphere of the psychological, may in that case be treated as a merely accidental factor in a new framework, in the context of which it can be made to appear as a troublesome superfluity. This is what happens in the writings of Lukács.

Lukács saw that a historical event like a revolution was charged with risk because it necessarily contained at the same time a dimension of theory and of practice. The force in a revolution turns not only against the existing relationships of production, and not only against those who have a direct interest in maintaining the specific structure of these relationships as their own. The force turns also against the members of that class in whose name the revolution is made. Lukács believed that the fate of the revolution depended on the ideological maturity of the proletariat. Yet he conceded that the proletariat 'is forced to seize power at a time and in a frame of mind in which it inwardly still perceives the bourgeois social order as the properly legal one'.[5] Nor did he deny that 'the proletariat in many ways still remains very strongly trapped in capitalist forms of thought and feeling';[6] so much so indeed that they undertake the task of social change 'with the mixture of vacillation and haste characteristic of the usurper', who 'inwardly, in thought, feeling and resolve, anticipates the inevitable restoration of capitalism'.[7] Hence the proletariat 'can only be liberated from its dependence upon the life-forms created by capitalism when it has learnt to act without these life-forms inwardly influencing its actions'.[8] Indeed, in *Taktik und Ethik* he went even further in arguing that not only parliamentary activity but the party of the proletariat itself was a concession to bourgeois reality. The party expressed externally the inner contradiction characteristic of the capitalist process of production in its current phase: for whereas the 'proletariat has become too strong to withdraw from political activity', it was nonetheless 'still not strong enough to be able to impose its will and interests on society'; and as a result 'the party of the proletariat was forced to acknowledge the form of capitalist society'. It criticises those forms in vain, in word and deed, while participating in elections, in parliamentary life, and so on. In this sense, 'it has in fact admitted capitalist society'.[9]

But precisely this insight into the 'embourgeoisement of the proletariat' remains without consequences for his further reflections in *History and Class Consciousness*. He knows very well that there is a difference between the empirical consciousness of the proletariat and what he sees as its world-historical role, whose accomplishment, he grants, is not guaranteed. But he then forcibly closes this gap. At this point he takes a decisive step when he asserts that a historical analysis must establish from the start 'the distance that separates class consciousness from the empirically given, and from the psychologically desirable and explicable ideas which men form about their situation in life';[10] so that class consciousness is 'not the psychological consciousness of individual proletarians or the mass-psychological consciousness of all of them, but the meaning of the historical position of the class which has become conscious'.[11] From this point onwards, the complex part played by the 'subjective factor' is something he would prefer to neglect. It is not simply that he becomes indifferent to the subjective element; he would simply like to conjure it out of existence. In order to do this he starts to talk in subjunctives. The correct consciousness of the proletariat, he tells us, is an awareness directed to the whole social structure; it would be those thoughts 'which men in a particular life-situation *would* have, *if they were able fully to comprehend* this situation'. So class consciousness is the 'rationally appropriate reaction . . . which in this way is *imputed* to a certain typical position in the process of production'.[12] And, lest we mistake his meaning, the essence of Marxism, he now contends, consists in 'the knowledge of the independence of the truly driving forces of history from the (psychological) consciousness of men concerning them'.[13] Since he does not want to wait for the realm of freedom to come, he bridges the gap which he clearly sees between the 'real' and the 'necessary' consciousness of the proletariat. For the theoretical problem he finds a political solution: the party. This closes the gap between reality and possibility; as the 'conscience of the historical mission of the proletariat', it acts as a superior court of appeal administering commands. The title of Lukács' collected essays, *History and Class Consciousness*, now emerges into a somewhat eerie light; both terms in this putative connection have become abstract.

'History' appears to play an almost ghostly role in his account. In most of the essays there is little reference to the real history of either the capitalist mode of production or the working class struggle, and the whole institutional substructure of bourgeois class power – parties, reformist trade unions, newspapers, schools, families – is rarely mentioned. 'Class Consciousness', the development of the proletariat's awareness, occupies a focal point in his analysis. Yet in the end Lukács' version of historical materialism presents us with a class consciousness which must not be the consciousness of real men, but one which begins to soar high over their heads. That which, in view of the supposed historical mission of the proletariat, is so crucial, has now been forced to sink to the level of an appendix: the 'subjective factor'. The train of Lukács' thought closes by undercutting its own impetus. The 'and' in the title not only links entities which have themselves become reified; it marks the point of a break. With the 'and' in *History and Class Consciousness* Lukács claims to offer a single central vision, one coherent organising principle in terms of which alone, so he believes, all that his essays say have significance. But this 'and' is the site of a profound rupture. In the world of allegory, the Proletariat, who are hardly yet aware of their historical role and still adhere to bourgeois values, is stylised into the Subject–Object of History. In the world of reality, the party undertakes the administration of its class consciousness, so guaranteeing that unity of Subject and Object which does not yet empirically exist. When at last Subject and Object are yoked by violence together, the casualty is the 'subjective' factor. Purportedly the focus of Lukács' historical dynamic, this now turns into a chameleon. Insofar as it is adapted to his metaphysics of History, it is the motor of History; insofar as it deviates from that, it is mere psychology.

Here is the point of intersection between the two angles present already in Marx, the concept of ideology and the concept of class. The intersection occurs at the nodal point where the subjective factor and the public sphere meet. It is here that the question posed earlier becomes urgent: what is the appropriate response when the development of new productive forces makes it possible to impede the formation of a critical public? The early writings of critical theory were addressed to this question. This led them to revise radically the terms of Marx's analysis. They recognised that the power of ideology extended beyond the reach of discursive propositions. They sought to investigate the ways in which the conditions and constraints of the capitalist process of production became *introjected* by those who are subject to its power.

Horkheimer and Adorno highlighted this problem in different ways. Horkheimer turned mainly towards the interaction between authoritarian drives within the familial microcosm and the social macrocosm. Adorno turned towards the distinction and interaction between sociological and psychological concepts, which was falsely perceived as a purely formal problem because the whole social network had stamped its imprint upon all academic distinctions.

Horkheimer recognises that material force alone does not suffice to explain why a dominated class keeps enduring the domination exercised over it; it is especially insufficient when the cultural world is evidently in a state of dissolution and the economic apparatus appears to be ripe for a better system of production. Nor would the disclosure of ideological concepts resolve the problem; 'in no way do mere ideological manoeuvres form the root at this historically important moment for the preservation of an obsolete social system'.[14] It is the psychic structure of the various social classes which is constantly renewed by their position within the economic process. If, therefore, 'men preserve relations which they have outgrown in force and need, instead of replacing them through a higher and more rational form of organisation', that is possible 'only because the actions of a numerically significant social strata are not determined by cognition, but by an instinctual motive force that falsifies consciousness'.[15] Instinctual constraints imprison the potential drives for liberation, innate in all men and women, in a tight net. Specifically, Horkheimer focuses on the family as the psychological agency of society. This cellular unit reproduces and reinforces the domination of the whole society; it is the indispensable microstructure for the macrostructure. The category of authority is crucial for understanding macrostructure and microstructure alike. Patriarchal authority is able to present a semblance of naturalness, by recourse to a twofold foundation. Physical strength is directly identified with 'estimability';[16] and since the husband earns and possesses the money, which is power in the form of 'substance', he is able to make wife, sons, and daughters 'his'.[17] Because of the separation in time and space between familial and professional life, 'every bourgeois father may in social life have a very modest position and have to bend the knee to others, yet at home he will be the master and exercise the highly important function of accustoming his children to discretion and obedience'.[18] When suspected of paternalism, the nicest paternalist instinctively reaches for his cane. Father is thus forced into crippling collusion with the capitalist process. Mother, meanwhile, is more or less quietly limited to a submissive role in which some of her vital needs are denied; to make this tolerable, she consecrates her curtailment as a sacrifice; and so for her part she helps to reinforce the circle of guilt by cherishing in her children the sense that this sacrifice must be shown, somehow, to have not been in vain. Within this first circle of the family, the children learn 'not to trace every failure back to its social causes but to remain at the level of the individual and hypostatise the failure in religious terms as sin or in naturalistic terms as deficient natural endowment'.[19] The capitalist class in the macrostructure are quick to draw profit from this; aware as they are of the value of the family as a generator of an authority-oriented cast of mind, they seek to strengthen the bonds of society through the bonds of the family – by outlawing extramarital sexual relations, by disseminating propaganda for having and rearing children, and by restricting women to the domestic sphere. The psychic surplus value accruing to the capitalist process is inflationary. The bad conscience of the individual, nurtured in the family, absorbs energies which might otherwise be directed against the social circumstances that play such a decisive role in the individual's failure; and a compulsive sense of guilt, taking the form of a continuous readiness to be sacrificed, renders fruitless any criticism of the real causes of the trouble. The mental world into which the child grows in consequence of such dependence is controlled 'by the thought of man's power over man, of above and below, of command and obedience'.[20] The seeming necessity of a hierarchical division of mankind becomes so obvious for the child that he can experience the social world, and the universe as a whole, only under this aspect; the hierarchical division of command and obedience is the pre-given mould into which every new impression is poured.

In diagnosing the interaction between the productive process and the individual psyche Horkheimer to some degree simplifies the problem by focusing attention almost exclusively on the microcosmic unit of the family. Adorno sets out to correct this oversimplification by widening the focus. His attention is trained not so much on any particular agency of authority as rather on the methodical problem which any critical theory of society has to face: that is, the problem of explaining the process of introjecting domination in general. The object of Adorno's critique is what he sees as the twin reductions of sociologism and psychologism.[21] Sociologism reduces society to a surface phenomenon by failing to penetrate society's reign over the psychic structure of all individuals; psychologism reduces social concepts and conditions to individual and psychological ones. On this view, both flatten out the society/individual antagonism, the former in favour of an abstract notion of 'society', the latter in favour of an abstract notion of the 'individual'. Further, all previous attempts to go beyond these complementary reductions, by seeking for mediating links between Marxist concepts and psychoanalytic concepts, have repeated the same failure in their own way. The problem which they expressly strove to solve was the relationship between productive processes and instinctual demands. This problem they sought to meet by maintaining a grasp on both sides of the difficulty. Yet the difference between the two sets of concepts which they enlisted, and tried to surpass by assimilation, led them again and again to a critical point where their proposed solutions fell short of the mark. Either they sought to define social conditions in primarily psychoanalytic terms; or they tried to define more specifically psychoanalytic matters in concepts proper to a theory of society. Adorno argues that the double failures of 'bourgeois' reductionism and 'Freudian–Marxist' synthesis echoed the same basic mistake. What they failed to recognise was that the difference between concepts and conditions referring to the productive process, on the one side, and concepts and conditions referring to psychoanalytic processes, on the other side, could never be properly seen, as a difference, if it was viewed as a methodological problem. Formal difficulties were insoluble at the formal level; in separation from specific, material, historical contexts they simply could not be approached. For in Adorno's view the difference is a historical, not a formal, one; and hence, as a distinction, it can never be resolved by thought alone. What is necessary for critical theory, rather, is to demonstrate the untruth of these concepts by first acknowledging their provisional truth. It is true that 'in the face of the present impotence of the individual – all individuals – what is primary in explaining social processes and tendencies in society are sciences concerned with society: sociology and economics'.[22] It is also true that 'since the market economy was shattered, and patched up provisionally until the next crisis, its laws do not suffice for its explanation; other than by psychology, in which the objective composition is continually and newly internalised, it is not understandable either why men passively adjust to a condition of unchanged destructive irrationality or why they enrol in movements whose contradiction to their own interests is in no way difficult to perceive'.[23] Unconditional acceptance of these two – partial – truths would reproduce their static, ahistorical, character, and so conceptually reproduce the prevailing order of things. Whereas provisional acceptance of the two partial truths would make it conceptually possible to surpass the particular form in which they have been handed down. A critical theory, conceived on these lines, would seek to establish a theory of subjectivity consciously indebted to Freudian psychoanalysis. In so doing it would demonstrate that 'Freudian psychology does not so much capitulate to the appearance of individuality as it fundamentally destroys it as only a philosophical and social concept can do'.[24] As a theory of the subjective it would succeed in being doubly objective. For it explores subjectivity until it rediscovers social determinants in the deepest layers of the psyche. And by this means it discloses a society that seeks to administer individuals, as unique subjects, out of existence. It is by this argument that Adorno seeks to demonstrate that inherited static concepts can be recuperated by turning them into dynamic ones, once it is acknowledged that the problem of the relation between productive processes and psychic processes is in reality a substantive question in a formal guise.

This substantive problem concerning the relation between productive processes and psychic processes becomes a préssing one not simply because it bears upon issues which had remained unresolved within Marx's apparatus of concepts. What makes these theoretical difficulties practically urgent is the development of two new formations in the capitalist process of production. It was this that precipitated new departures from Marx. The point of critical entry for uncovering ideological deformations had become more rightly barred.

For critical theory the fact of fascism was a definitive experience. Hence it can hardly be surprising that they inclined to see international capitalism through the lens of German fascism. This made their insights both more acute and more obscure. The mote in their left eyes became a magnifying glass, and the specific differences between totalitarianism and monopoly capitalism tended to collapse into a one-dimensional vision.[25]

But German fascism and monopoly capitalism did indeed have one characteristic in common. Both violated territorial limits by crushing down the boundary lines between the so-called public and private spheres characteristic of the liberal epoch in Western Europe. This changed the nature and scope of ideology. If we think of ideology as a system of distorted communication extending between two poles – the transmission of messages and its reception by addressees – both poles had become transformed.

The change is apparent, first of all, in the nature of the messages. Adorno has explained this difference between the old and the new ideology succinctly. The old ideology is 'a consciousness which is objectively necessary and yet at the same time false ... which is just as distinct from the whole truth as it is from the pure lie'; as such it belongs 'to a developed urban market economy. For ideology is justification. It presupposes the experience of a societal condition which has already become problematical and therefore requires a defence.'[26] The new ideology, on the other hand, no longer betrays such necessity for apologetics. It is more 'a manipulative contrivance, a mere instrument of power, which actually no one, not even those who used it themselves, ever believed or expected to be taken seriously'.[27] The methods of persuasion characteristic of fascist propaganda aimed at winning people over by playing upon their unconscious mechanisms rather than by presenting ideas and arguments. 'It does not employ discursive logic but is rather ... what might be called an organised flight of ideas. The relation between premises and inferences is replaced by a linking-up of ideas resting on mere similarity, often through association by employing the same characteristic word in two propositions which are logically quite unrelated. This method not only evades the control mechanisms of rational examination, but also makes it psychologically easier for the listener to "follow". He has no exacting thinking to do, but can give himself up passively to a stream of words in which he swims.'[28] Hence the critique of such ideologies cannot see its task as that of refuting them, since political programmes and even specific political ideas play only a minor role compared with the psychological stimuli applied to the audience. The new critique needs to analyse, rather, the devices used for the programming of affects, for it is this which determines what pieces of information are assimilated and what others are blocked out from the range of attention. Among such devices for the programming of affective responses, personalisation, gratification and stereotyping play a prominent part. Fascist propaganda is personalised, in the sense that the agitators spend a large part of their time in speaking about themselves or about their audiences; they identify themselves with their listeners and lay particular emphasis upon being simultaneously both modest little men and leaders of great calibre.[29] It offers gratification, in the sense that propaganda functions as wish-fulfilment. 'People are "let-in", they are supposedly getting the inside dope, taken into confidence, treated as of the elite who deserve to know the lurid mysteries hidden from outsiders.'[30] The audience's gratitude for this 'show' is enhanced by a particular kind of emotional break-through; for although the showmen 'resemble their listeners in most respects', the fascist leaders 'differ from them in an important one: they know no inhibitions in expressing themselves. They function vicariously for their inarticulate listeners by doing and saying what the latter would like to, but either cannot or dare not. They violate the taboos which middle-class society has put upon any expressive behaviour on the part of the normal, matter-of-fact citizen.'[31] And finally, fascist propaganda produces a hypnotic effect by means of its stereotypes. 'The similarity of the utterances of various agitators' is so great that it is enough in principle to 'analyse the statements of one of them in order to know them all'; 'the speeches themselves are so monotonous that one meets with endless repetitions as soon as one is acquainted with the very limited number of stock devices'; and in fact 'constant reiteration and scarcity of ideas are indispensable ingredients of the entire technique'.[32] What Adorno has analysed in the specific case of fascist propaganda discloses, with some variations, the features of a more general historical trend. Both political propaganda and marketing psychology reach down into private areas of individual life to exploit personal conflicts or to waken artificial needs in support of a particular system. By blurring the distinction between the private and the institutionalised, they make it more difficult to separate internal desire and external suggestion. The superstructure is more firmly anchored in the individual substructure. It was this which highlighted the new capacity of ideologies to dispense with systems of explanatory concepts. It was clearly possible to reduce the ideological distance between concepts and the circumstances to which concepts referred: precisely that ideological distance within which Marx's classic ideology-critique had moved.

The second pole in this system of distorted communication, the status of the addressee, is transformed correspondingly. The reader of the printed word had enjoyed the privilege of a particular distance from the message which was transmitted to him; this distance was required by the privacy of assimilation, and it fostered the emergence of a public who engaged in rational discussion of what they had read. But the new media of radio, film and television tend to break down this critical distance; in this sense, their effect is more penetrative than that of the press could ever have been. It has been rightly said that television and radio, because they appear, among all of the media, to have the most direct line of communication to individuals, are perhaps the most influential. At its best the newspaper exerts a tremendously powerful influence; and yet it is less personalised than the media of broadcasting, pictures and films, and certainly less intimate in concept. The press, however, allows for privacy of thought, for only one person can read a speech in a newspaper, but several may watch and listen to it. 'A televised speech is directed electronically "to you", the listener. The same speech reprinted in the morning paper is one step removed from immediacy and directness.'[33] Thus in comparison with printed communications, the specific characteristics of the new media have the effect of curtailing the reflective reactions of the receiver to the material transmitted. They are able to draw the public as listeners and viewers within their power; and yet at the same time they deprive them of the distance of their autonomy, that is, the chance of being able to pause to go back over the sequence of messages, to speak back and contradict. By curtailing this possibility of critical distance, the incursion of the electronic media into the intimate sphere of what was previously the realm of privacy creates a new kind of public world. The social framework of the traditional forms in which political opinions were formed – the Agora, the Forum, the Court, the assembly of the estates, the parliament – is now, as it were, dissolved into the private living-room. The addressee of the new communication systems is not formally located; he can be found everywhere and nowhere. He is addressed in contexts in which he is released from the duty of representing a role for the public for which he could be held responsible: the new media impart messages to addressees who feel relieved of their public responsibility. But if politics is understood as a sphere of activity and a set of formal arrangements which foster responsible action on matters concerning the community as a whole, it follows that this new public must be described as unpolitical. Empirical social research into public opinion more or less unwittingly corroborates this change, while refraining from any critical reflection on its implications.[34] By bracketing out the institutional aspects of the problem, it dissolves the concept of public opinion into a social–psychological analysis of group processes. Thus we are told in a standard text on the topic that 'public opinion refers to people's attitudes on an issue when they are members of the same social group'.[35] This definition makes clear what decades of empirical progress have eliminated from the concept of public opinion. Both terms, 'public' and 'opinion', have been reduced in meaning. The 'public', as the subject of public opinion, has come to be equated with 'group', as the social–psychological substratum of a process of communication between two or more individuals; the term 'group' abstracts from a whole host of assumptions, and in particular from the network of institutional arrangements specifically designed to make possible the alliance of private individuals so that they could form a politically effective, reasoning public capable of exercising critical surveillance over the activities of the executive power. And the concept of 'opinion' has been subjected to a corresponding reduction. At first empirical social research identified opinion with 'expression on a controversial topic';[36] later, with 'expression of an attitude';[37] then simply with 'attitude';[38] and later still, the concept was widened and diffused to include any kind of habitual response which is expressed in ideas – precisely, in fact, those opinions bearing the stamp of what used to be religion, custom and prejudice, against which the eighteenth-century notion of public opinion was contrasted and to which it was critically opposed. In the end, empirical social research viewed opinion as something which did not even need to be capable of verbalisation but could include modes of behaviour as such; such behaviour earns the attribute of publicity solely through its connection with group processes. In this way the social–psychological reduction of the notion of public opinion performed by empirical social research duplicates the structural change in the nature of the new ideology. It becomes itself an ideological reflex.

What emerges from this analysis is a perspective on the contemporary situation in which two concepts of public opinion are locked in competition. The one views it as a potentially critical agency, required by the publicity which is necessary for the proper control and surveillance of the executive power. The other views it as really a receptive organ, developed through organisation over the heads and behind the backs of the public, the 'engineering of consent'[39] for the demonstrative purpose of surrounding particular persons, institutions, consumer goods and political programmes with an aura of acclamation, prestige and good will. There is an observable historical trend for this second view of public opinion to gain ground at the expense of the first. The term public opinion is used to refer to the manipulation of the public at least to the same extent as it is used to refer to a process of scrutiny by the public. Critical publicity has come to be challenged and to a considerable degree supplanted by manipulated publicity. In this situation critical theory reinterpreted the meaning of ideology-critique. It is seen as having a specifically new task: the task of analysing those mechanisms which tend to dissolve that critical public on the existence of which Marx's original ideology-critique was based.

4

The dialectic of enlightenment

At the threshold of the thirties, European society was in the throes of a crisis which seemed to demonstrate the self-destructive tendency inherent in capitalism and the impotence of liberal democracy. The choice appeared to lie between fascism and communism. Critical theorists were thus able to view their work at the outset as part of a revolutionary political struggle. Yet from the beginning their practical role in this context was obscure. Horkheimer's understanding of critical theory was never articulated in any specific form of political organisation; and by 1932 he had set the tone for a major reorientation of the Institute for Social Research at Frankfurt, when it ceased to issue the *Archives for the History of Socialism and the Workers' Movement* and brought out a new review with the politically more innocuous title, *The Journal of Social Research*. Horkheimer's first crystallisation of his position was thus not so much the assumption of an unequivocal revolutionary standpoint as rather the expression of revulsion against capitalist oppression and against the denial of that oppression by the prevailing ideology. But just as he was adopting this position any possibility that might have existed of establishing organisational links with the working class of his own country were eliminated by the Nazi seizure of power. Fascism directly destroyed those social forces which had appealed to Marxism, by producing a counter-revolutionary solution to the crisis of capitalism the possibility of which had not been foreseen by classical Marxism. Gradually it came to appear, especially to emigrés in an alien culture, that the catastrophes of the thirties were the turbulent beginning of a long-term development which could continue further in more peaceful forms; fascism now appeared as a violent episode in the transition to corporate capitalism. Finally, the mass extermination in the concentration camps and the enormous destruction of men and material in the Second World War caused Horkheimer's initial revulsion against capitalism to freeze into a traumatic experience at once more emotionally intense and more conceptually diffused: as if mankind as a whole, with the aid of its gigantic technological apparatus, were inexorably heading towards an inferno – a sado-masochistic vision of history which was in itself no novelty, but re-echoed the fascination exerted by the nihilistic potential of technology evident among a number of thinkers in the German language-area during the first quarter of this century.

This change was registered in the joint work by Horkheimer and Adorno, *Dialectic of Enlightenment*. Its distance from critical theory as initially elaborated is evident both in its formal structure and in its substantive propositions.

The formal change breaks down the differentiation of Hork-heimer's initial research project. His original version of critical theory sought to focus the study of domination by pursuing three interrelated levels of analysis: the economic system, the psychic disposition of social groups, and the theory of culture. To a large extent this remained a programme. It is true that the collaborative work *Studien über Autorität und Familie* sought to show how authoritarianism was inculcated within the family unit; that the five-volume collective work, *Studies in Prejudice*, presented the results of investigations into the human forces which are mobilised whenever totalitarian movements, particularly in the form of race hatred, assume a sizeable form; and that scattered components of a theory of late capitalism appeared in articles by Kirchheimer and Neumann in the *Zeitschrift für Sozialforschung*. But after the *Zeitschrift* ceased to appear in 1941 critical theory as jointly represented by Horkheimer and Adorno assumed a radically new form. Had they continued the intentions of the original programme they would have addressed sharply pointed questions to contemporary historical developments: questions concerning the economic, social–psychological, and cultural grounds for the transformation of the Weimar Republic into Fascism, and for the emergence in Russia of Stalinist domination. Instead of this, the inquiry becomes raised to a level of abstraction where world history as a whole is taken as its theme. In this they are quite explicit: 'We had set ourselves nothing less than the discovery of why mankind, instead of entering into a truly human condition, is sinking into a new kind of barbarism.'[1] The differentiation of the original inquiry into political economy, social psychology and cultural theory is diffused, and re-tied in the knot of an obscurely encoded philosophy of history. It is no accident that the book should bear the subtitle 'Philosophical Fragments'; that, unlike Marx's critiques, it consists not of a single consequent argument but of a series of mutually referential essays; and that the last of these essays is followed by a further fifty pages of shorter notes and sketches. The structure of the work enacts a process of disintegration.

The substantive change breaks down Horkheimer's original faith in the potentially liberating capacities of science and technology. In his early writings he had taken the view that the humane function of science depended on its humane application. The scientific mode of thought and its products are neither humane nor inhumane; the attribute of humanity can only be meaningfully applied or denied them in terms of the way in which they are practically used. Nevertheless, their liberating potential was seen as enormous: scientific method belongs to 'precisely those forces which are working for the betterment of the human situation'.[2] For the domination of nature which is possible only through the development of the natural sciences is an indispensable precondition of true human freedom. Only the control of nature guarantees what ultimately matters: the 'rational planning' of a world in need of coherent organisation.[3] But in *Dialectic of Enlightenment* the domination of nature through science and technology becomes the object of critique. The fact that rational control over nature which has grown with the European philosophical and technological achievement has produced such anti-human results is seen, not as the consequence of historically contingent factors, but as necessarily resulting from that achievement itself. 'Even the deductive form of science,' it is now claimed, 'reflects hierarchy and coercion'; for 'just as the first categories represented the organised tribe and its power over the individual, so the whole logical order, dependency, connection, progression, and union of concepts is grounded in the corresponding conditions of social reality',[4] that is, its division of labour. Thus every attempt to break subjection to the domination of nature, 'because nature is broken, enters all the more deeply into that natural enslavement'.[5] The Enlightenment is said to have changed into positivism;[6] to serve capital;[7] to become totalitarian;[8] and to culminate in fascism.[9]

It would be wrong to view the formal and substantive changes expressed in *Dialectic of Enlightenment* simply as the response to an impasse made evident by the historical developments of the thirties and forties. If those developments exerted so radical an impact on the whole structure of the theory that was only possible because of a deficiency which had been present in that theory from the very outset. The direction taken by critical theory since its inception is not so much the precipitate of historical circumstances external to it, as rather the working out of assumptions latent in its initial formulation. This may be demonstrated by elaborating the implications contained in two propositions which were central to Horkheimer's position as set out in his programmatic essay of 1937. He there states that 'in recognising the present form of economy and the whole culture which it generates to be the product of human work as well as the organisation which mankind was capable of and has provided for itself in the present era', critical theorists 'identify themselves with this totality and conceive it as will and reason'.[10] And elsewhere he claims that this whole process aims at a freedom which is 'identical with the control of nature in us and outside us through rational decision'.[11] There is a certain indeterminancy in these two formulations, but they contain nonetheless a distinct tendency, which is reinforced by the basic thrust of the whole essay. All social reality is subsumed under one category: it is to be understood as the product of work.

This means that no distinction is clearly made in principle between control over nature and control over social relationships. The failure to clarify that distinction has serious consequences, both for the conception of an emancipated society, and for the critique of existing society.

Horkheimer sees critical theory as directed by an interest which is not arbitrarily attached to it but is a constituent part of the theory itself. It 'quite consciously pursues an interest in a rational organisation of human activity which it has set itself to elucidate and legitimise. For it is not just concerned with goals as they have been prescribed by the existing life forms, but with men and all their possibilities.'[12] Mankind's full possibilities could be realised only in 'an association of free men in which each has the same possibility of self-development'.[13] This form of social life does not yet exist because of the opposition between the prevailing irrationality of social relations and 'the individual's inherent rationality'.[14] Since 'activity governed by reason is proper to men',[15] existing social conditions are inhuman. The judgement that present conditions are inhuman because they fall short of the goal of a rational form of social organisation must be more than an ideal which is arbitrarily imposed in evaluating present society, for otherwise it could not avoid the reproach of being utopian. Horkheimer explicitly dismisses this charge by arguing that the goal is implicit in every human activity and that it can be perceived as a historical tendency. The association of free men which critical theory is able to envisage 'is not an abstract utopia, for the possibility in question can be shown to be real even at the present stage of productive forces'.[16] There now exists a 'possibility that men would become aware of and make as their goal the path which the social work process has taken',[17] without that path having so far been directed by any definite theory. This inherent tendency cannot attain its goal by blind necessity; 'a certain interest is also required if these tendencies are to be perceived and expressed'.[18] Critical theory has the specific task of identifying this latent tendency and so making it amenable to conscious direction. The claim that critical theory has an interest in human emancipation is therefore not the expression of an abstract ideal but can be justified. 'The viewpoints which critical theory derives from historical analysis as the goals of human activity, especially the idea of a rational organisation of society that will meet the needs of the whole community, are immanent in human work.'[19]

Horkheimer's failure to distinguish between control over nature and control over social relations also affects his critique of the prevailing society. He focuses his critique of capitalism upon the fact that an irrational whole results from the rational, planned action of isolated individuals. This irrational whole is subject to no plan but is regulated only by uncomprehended social forces, which issue in periodically recurrent catastrophes. Within the framework of capitalism men experience the fact that society is comparable to 'nonhuman natural processes, to pure mechanisms, because cultural forms which are supported by war and oppression are not the creations of a unified, self-conscious will'.[20] The social nexus of capitalism appears primarily, in this analysis, in its negative aspect, that is as an anarchy of production. Its positive aspect, the law of value, is not explicitly reflected upon as such. This entails an important displacement of accent in the understanding of reification, in contrast with Marx's critique. The fact that reification, viewed here as the illusory objectivity of a mechanism which appears to operate by its own independent laws, arises on the basis of a specific social formation – that is, the structuring of the work process by the exploitation built into the particular institution of surplus-value – here remains unexpressed. The tendency to subsume all human activity under one category, to derive it from the single principle of work, founders on the fact that human interaction takes particular forms in specific social formations by means of antagonistic social relationships. The concept of work becomes for Horkheimer an ontological category, it designates the primary process. The result is that it is used in so generalised a way that, although the existence of social antagonisms is of course mentioned, no adequate basis is provided for producing a really differentiated account of specific forms of social domination. The serious limitations of this approach become evident once it becomes necessary to give some account of the transition from 'anarchic' to 'organised' capitalism. Given Horkheimer's starting point, this transition must come to be seen as the extension of the rationality represented earlier by isolated individuals to the whole of society. On the other hand, it becomes evident that organised capitalism has little in common with the supposed realm of freedom, which earlier had been hoped for from the increasing rationalisation of social relations. The only way out of the difficulty – if, as is the case, a return to a specifically economic critique continues to be avoided – is to make the critique more radical: that is, to turn it against the criterion on which it had been previously based – the model of rational action derived from the work process.

This is what happened in *Dialectic of Enlightenment*. Domination is not now seen as arising from any specific social formation. The relationship between man and nature in itself necessitates and perpetuates domination, irrespective of whatever organisational structures predominate at any particular time. 'Men have always had to choose between their subjection to nature or the subjection of nature to the self.'[21] The domination of nature develops from an 'inescapable compulsion';[22] and its result, 'the principle of the self', becomes 'the evolutionary law of society'.[23] This historical process is therefore not contingent but inevitable. It executes a trajectory which marks the passage from the condition of myth to the condition of enlightenment. Neither 'myth' nor 'enlightenment' refer here to world-views alone; the whole of social life – the forces of production and distribution, the psychic disposition of men, and all their cultural forms – are subsumed under these two categories.

Enlightenment comes to regard nature as an object amenable to transformation by men. To do this it must eliminate the basic principle of myth. This is the principle of anthropomorphism, the projection on to nature of the subjective. In this view, the supernatural, spirits and demons, are mirror images of men who allow themselves to be frightened by natural phenomena. Consequently the many mythic figures can all be referred back to a common denominator, and reduced to the human subject.[24] The aim of this reduction is to free men from the dangers of natural existence, both animal and vegetative, and to protect them, at ever higher levels of enlightenment, from the fear of reversion to a more archaic condition of subjection to the sway of natural forces. All natural residues in man must be eliminated from this new concept of the self; it must be no longer either body or blood, or soul, or even the natural I; the self, once sublimated into the transcendental or logical subject, becomes the reference point of reason.[25] And all external nature must be stripped of qualities, for to eliminate qualities is to get rid of the remaining vestiges of anthropomorphism; the dissimilar must be made comparable by reducing it to abstract quantities; and that which cannot be reduced to numbers becomes illusion.[26] The unity of the rational subject confronts the unity of inanimate nature. There is now a single relation between the subject who bestows meaning and the meaningless object. This entails the renunciation of mimesis. Mimetic modes of behaviour, that is imitative actions in the broadest sense of the word, were acts of empathy with natural forces. The forces of nature were viewed as possible partners in interaction; a form of communicative dialogue was considered possible which allowed the person to open himself up to the other subjectivities contained in nature by a process of playful or ritualised 'assimilation'. The magician imitates demons; in order to frighten them or appease them he behaves frighteningly or makes gestures of appeasement.[27] The suppression of anthropomorphism goes hand in hand with the suppression of this mimetic impulse. Because in the view of enlightenment it is no longer possible to see nature as a subject, it also becomes meaningless to preserve communicative modes of behaviour in relation to it. A successful relation with nature can be achieved not by way of communicative interaction but only by control through instrumental transformation. The process culminates in the conquest of external nature which must be perpetually exploited in order to yield to human needs.

The exploitation of external nature for the purpose of freeing men from subjection to it strikes back in the repression of man's instinctual nature. Nature – his own as well as that of the external world – is 'given' to the ego as something that has to be fought and conquered. This means that, in the interest of self-preservation, the self is engaged in constant inner struggle to repress many of its own natural drives. The strain of holding the ego together in this way adheres to it in all stages; and the temptation to lose it has always been present together with the determination to maintain it. This dread of losing the self, which in its extreme form figures as the fear of death and destruction is, nonetheless, intimately associated with 'a promise of happiness, which threatened civilisation in every moment'.[28] That promise must therefore be suppressed. The intellect must separate itself off from sensuous experience in order to subjugate it. But this coercive separation inevitably impoverishes human potentialities. All progress in instrumental control must pay the price of regression in affective experience. 'Mankind, whose versatility and knowledge become differentiated with the division of labour, is at the same time forced back to anthropologically more primitive stages, for with the technical easing of life the persistence of domination brings about a fixation of the instincts by means of heavier repression.'[29] Imagination atrophies in the struggle. The struggle begins with the perpetual internal conquest of the 'lower' faculties of the individual, his sensuous and appetitive capacities. At least since Plato, their subjugation is regarded as a necessary element of human reason, which is thus in its very function repressive. The struggle culminates in a productive system whose maintenance requires that the human body be subordinated to its needs. Thus the impairment of the workers' experience is not simply 'a stratagem of the rulers', but the 'logical consequence' of a technological society in which the very course of the effort to escape the subjection to external nature inevitably leads to the subjection of internal nature.[30] This is why the transition from the condition of myth to the condition of enlightenment is not linear but dialectical. 'The curse of irresistible progress is irresistible regression.'[31]

Horkheimer and Adorno seek to demonstrate the necessary connection between irresistible progress and irresistible regression by a reinterpretation of the Homeric fable of Odysseus. No work, they claim, provides more eloquent testimony than that of Homer, 'the basic text of European civilization', of 'the mutual implication of enlightenment and myth';[32] and in the *Odyssey*, 'one of the earliest representative testimonies of Western bourgeois civiliza- tion',[33] they find the model for the pre-history of the bourgeois subject.

The voyage of Odysseus from Troy to Ithaca is the way taken through the myths by the self – always physically weaker as against the power of nature. The adventures of Odysseus are all dangerous temptations removing the self from its logical course and threaten- ing it with destruction. He is always physically weaker than the primitive powers with which he must struggle for his life. Because of this, he can never engage in direct conflict with mythic forces but has always to acknowledge the status of the sacrificial ceremonies by which they are appeased. He dare not contravene them. For each of the mythic figures is programmed always to do the same thing; each is a figure of repetition and compulsion; each rep- resents some facet of the cycle of nature within which man is bound. The fact that it was impossible for Odysseus to choose any route other than that between Scylla and Charybdis may be viewed as a mythic representation of the superior power of the currents over the small, antique ships. But in this mythic tradition the natural relation of strength and impotence has assumed the form of a legal condition. Scylla and Charybdis have a right to what comes between them. Odysseus opposes this situation; he pits the integrity of his ego against the inevitability of natural fate. But he cannot defy the power of the Sirens directly; it is impossible to hear their song and not to succumb to them. This he already knows, for he has been warned by Circe, the divinity personifying reversion to the animal state, that whoever is lured by their promise of happiness will fall for their trickery and so perish. So Odysseus must seek to escape the legal conditions which restrict him, while strictly observing the letter of the law. He wants to discover a formula for rendering to nature what is nature's, and yet betray it in the very process. He must find an arrangement by which he as a subject need not be subjected to it. This he does by a double strategic act of force. One possibility he reserves for himself. He listens, but while bound impotently to the mast; the greater the temptation, the more he has his bonds tightened. He has found an escape clause in the contract, which enables him to fulfil it while eluding it; the contract has not provided for the possibility that the seafarer might listen bound or unbound. The other possibility he prescribes for his men. He plugs their ears with wax, and they must row with all their strength. They are able to survive because they are unable to hear. What Odysseus hears is without consequences for him – it becomes an object of contemplation, a work of art – while his men, who do not listen, leave him at the mast, thus saving him and themselves. In this way they 'reproduce the oppressor's life together with their own, and the oppressor is no longer able to escape his social role'.[34] Odysseus has found a stratagem for resisting the temptation while listening to it, and so is able to control the power of nature: but only at the price of doing violence to his own inner nature, and of establishing social domination. He must forcibly restrain his instinctual drives (he is bound to the mast); and he must force obedience upon those who travel with him (they must row), which in turn is only possible because he deludes them (he plugs their ears).[35]

Odyssean artifice has its prototype in the deception of archaic sacrifices. All his stratagems take place against the background of sacrifice to natural deities; and all human sacrifices, when systematically executed, aim to deceive the god to whom they are made; they seek to dissolve his power by subjecting him to the primacy of human ends.[36] Equally, Odyssean cunning is the prototype of bourgeois renunciation. The possibility he reserves for himself foreshadows the later strategy of the bourgeoisie, who 'deny themselves happiness all the more doggedly as it drew closer to them with the growth of their own power'.[37] And the possibility he imposes on his men foreshadows the later fate of labourers, who must 'doggedly sublimate in additional effort the drive that impels to diversion'.[38]

At the midpoint in this reading are the notions of sacrifice and renunciation. Odyssean artifice is a figure marking the transition from the one to the other. Horkheimer and Adorno believe that this historical transition is not accidental but inevitable. They claim that it is possible to derive from magical thinking itself a counter-principle to the mythic illusion of magical domination over nature. This is because sacrifice has a dual character. In one of its aspects, it is the magical self-surrender of the individual to the collective. In its other aspect, it is self-preservation by the technique of this magic. This dual character of sacrifice implies an objective contradiction which tends to the development of the rational element in sacrifice; the element of self-preservation gradually takes predominance over the element of self-surrender.[39]

Originally, the individual is credited with the capacity of magical representation: the blood of the slaughtered member of a tribe would flow back into the collective body of the tribe as energy. At one stage of pre-history, sacrifice as self-surrender marked an actual state of affairs required by the dominant form of reason. At times the collective, once its numbers had reached a certain level, could survive only by eating human flesh; and such customs of later periods by which in times of hunger an entire age group of youths was ritually required to emigrate bear unmistakable traces of such barbaric rationality. But once the systematised hunt began to provide the tribe with enough animals to make the consumption or expulsion of one's fellow tribesmen superfluous, the enlightened hunters and trappers must have been confused by the medicine man's command to surrender themselves as food. A growing sense of the irrational element in sacrifice – the self-surrender of the individual – develops when it is seen as no longer an appropriate means towards the end of controlling natural forces.[40]

The 'self' is the individual who is no longer credited with the capacity of magical representation. Abandoning sacrificial rites which threaten its own ego-boundaries, the identically persistent self frees itself from the threat of dissolution by opposing its cognitive faculties to nature and so gaining rational control over its environment. But the self is still imprisoned in the natural context as an organism that seeks to assert itself against the organic; and this natural context in which it remains enclosed includes its own natural drives as well as environmental constraints. The enmity of the self to sacrifice therefore entails a 'sacrifice' of part of the self, inasmuch as it is achieved only at the price of denying natural human drives for the sake of controlling external natural forces. Man's domination over himself, which grounds his selfhood, is inevitably a paradoxical achievement: it involves the mutilation of the subject in whose service it is undertaken. This self-denial for the sake of self-assertion is 'the nucleus of all civilizing rationality'.[41]

Thus although the principle of sacrifice is transient because of its irrationality – the element of self-surrender – it persists by virtue of its rationality – the element of self-preservation.[42] Its rationality has not disappeared but has been transformed, into renunciation. The central thought of Horkheimer and Adorno is the *introjection of sacrifice*. External ritual sacrifices as cults are superseded by internal instinctual sacrifices as constraints. Only in this way is the formation of an identical self possible in the struggle to subjugate nature, the subject of civilisation educated by a chain of renunciations, a self which constantly gives more than it receives in order to secure its own life. 'The irrationalism of totalitarian capitalism, whose way of satisfying needs has an objective form determined by domination which makes the satisfaction of needs impossible and tends toward the extermination of mankind, has its prototype in the hero who escapes from sacrifice by sacrificing himself. The history of civilisation is the history of the introversion of the sacrifice. In other words: the history of renunciation.'[43]

This dialectic of enlightenment is a dynamic process which appears to allow no exit. The ego which strives for external security and inner stability cannot be secure and stable as long as it is confronted by a resistant nature. The process of establishing distance from nature through control, which makes the identical self possible in the first place, is again and again the source of a fear of nature; yet this fear can only be alleviated through renewed control which must conceal its origins in fear. The process of growing domination exercised by the rational subject, in which the superiority of nature over men is worn away, is bought at the price of the increasing inflation of a 'second nature', an ever more impenetrable straitjacket of social and psychic coercions. The hope of enlightenment resigns itself to a vision of hopelessness, and the thought of an alternative practice shrinks to the recognition of its impossibility. The *Dialectic of Enlightenment* is a vicious circle, the historical inevitability of a *huis clos*.

The main problem with the argument advanced in *Dialectic of Enlightenment* concerns its concept of domination. This concept is vulnerable to criticism because it is applied in such a way as to impose crippling restrictions on the construction of a theory of society. The nature of the difficulty can best be brought out by a comparison with Marx's critique.

Horkheimer and Adorno share Marx's starting-point in two ways. They ask the same question, and they accept the same initial premise from which to set out their answer. Because they are convinced that 'social freedom is inseparable from enlightened thought',[44] they must try to discover why it is that, in spite of the Enlightenment, 'mankind, instead of entering into a truly human condition, is sinking into a new kind of barbarism'.[45] Marx also wants to save the essence of the Enlightenment from its romantic critics and so his critique, although he did not explicitly formulate it in this way, may be seen as an answer to the same question: why is it that rational control over nature which has grown out of the European philosophical achievement and has led to its technological achievement has nevertheless produced such anti-human results? And Marx also takes as his premise the fundamental distinction between man and nature in which nature is viewed as material amenable to transformation in order to produce certain results. Labour, the appropriation of natural substance to human requirements, 'is the general condition of the metabolism between men and nature; and it is the everlasting nature-imposed condition of human existence and therefore is independent of every social form of that existence, or rather, is common to every such form'.[46] For Marx this metabolism between man and nature is independent of any of its historical forms because it can be traced back to pre-social conditions: 'as the expression and maintenance of life, it is common both to the man who is not in any way socialised and to the man who is in some way socially determined'.[47]

It is at this point that they diverge. Marx differs from the authors of *Dialectic of Enlightenment* because he refers the man/nature relationship *directly to the dimension of intersubjectivity* within the framework of which it is organised. This leads him both to a different concept of self-formation and to a different understanding of domination.

Marx's view of self-formation is indebted to the post-romantic concept of expression, where expression means the bringing into existence of significant reality. On this view, man does not investigate and describe, by an appropriate method, a given order of affairs. He himself creates that order, rather as an artist creates a work of art; not by imitating pre-existing models or applying pre-existing rules, but rather by an original act of creation, the introduction into the world of a new element. This is what Marx means when he says that all past materialism has failed to grasp the fact that external material objects are the materialisations of human activity; that the object, 'reality', must be understood as the self-externalisation of a creative subject. This notion of externalisation, as the expression of an essence, is cast in a non-dualist form, such that the essence cannot be said to be until it has been expressed in external reality. By transforming external nature man constructs his own nature; when he 'objectifies' his creative potentialities through his transactions with the world of things, he grows in the consciousness of his own humanity, because he is able to see these things as the materialisations of his own projects. This position makes it possible for Marx to break through a logical impasse in the view of history that had been propounded by the materialist philosophers of the Enlightenment. The impasse arose from the contradiction between their humanism and their determinism; that is to say the arbitrary superimposition of an optimistic theory of historical progress upon a passive epistemology derived from Locke. Their belief that men were the objects of corrupting influences provided no means of showing how men could be prepared to reshape the corrupting institutions that had moulded them. As Marx put it, their doctrine that men are the product of circumstances and that, consequently, different men are the product of different circumstances, forgets the crucial point that it is men who educate themselves, that it is men who change these circumstances. The collective self-education of men through their own activity is a self-change. But this self-change is intrinsically social, for man's nature is a generic nature. Human nature is one essence shared by all individuals, a common life which they all share. The clue to their re-education is for mankind to reappropriate his own generic nature – to recover control of man's transformative activity. Human nature is made through social production.

What makes the man/nature relationship a problem for Marx, therefore, is the way in which it is socially organised. As long as the work process is viewed only as a process of interaction between man and nature, its simple elements remain the same in all social forms of development. For all epochs of production have certain characteristics in common because in all epochs the subject, the human species, and the object, nature, are the same. Thus nothing is easier than to obliterate the distinction between different forms of production by emphasis on their common characteristics. Marx's whole theoretical enterprise was directed to discovering the particular laws which regulate the rise, existence, development and demise of a given productive structure and its replacement by another, higher structure. For every particular historical stage of the productive process develops further the material base and the social forms, and his critique is concerned precisely with these social forms – as distinct from the nature-given content. The investigation of these specific social forms requires a process of abstraction quite different from that contained in *Dialectic of*

Enlightenment. The fundamental distinction in Marx's economic analysis is between 'capital in general' and 'the many aspects of capital'.[48] The first two volumes of *Capital* deal exclusively with 'capital in general'. This concept of capital in general excludes consideration of competition between elements of capital. Competition does not create the laws of the capitalist economy but merely embodies them; it does not explain them but only makes them visible. Nothing would be more misleading, therefore, than to confuse the investigation of these laws with the analysis of competition – precisely the confusion contained in Horkheimer's early stress on the 'anarchy of production'. In order to be able to investigate the immanent laws of capital in their pure form, it is necessary to abstract from competition and its accompanying manifestations and to start by analysing 'capital in general'. But what are the characteristics common to all aspects of capital? Clearly, they are those which pertain only to capital, but not to other forms of wealth. Capital differs from money or from mere value primarily because it is 'value which produces surplus-value', and this in turn is based on a specific social relationship – the relationship of wage labour. It is clear that in all class societies the surplus product generated by the direct producers is appropriated by the dominant class. But the difference between distinct forms of production is constituted precisely by whether this takes place in the form of slave-work, serfdom, or wage labour. Thus for Marx 'society' – the sphere of production, distribution and consumption – is always constituted in an intersubjective context of action. Just as there is no 'production in general' but only a form of production under specific social conditions, so there is no 'society in general' but only specific 'social formations' – the particular structures within which the conditions of production are organised. Marx distinguishes five such social formations: archaic society, slave-owning society, feudal society, capitalist society, and communist society. 'Social formation' is the basic term in the conceptual arsenal of historical materialism. Thus although Marx sees nature as material which is transformed by men, the relationship to nature is in no sense viewed by him directly as a form of 'domination' which turns in some unclear yet automatic process into social domination. Domination for Marx only has meaning in critical reference to the way in which the control over nature is socially organised. It refers to the contradiction between social production and private appropriation. In this sense domination is for Marx a derivative category: it must be traced back to a disharmony between the conditions of man's self-formative action, social production, and the constraints of class formation, private appropriation.

But in *Dialectic of Enlightenment* domination is the central category in establishing the relationship between man and nature. Social domination is seen as originating from the process whereby the subject establishes its identity by distancing itself from enclosure within nature. The peculiarity of this point of departure for constructing a theory of domination lies in the suggestion of derivation: social domination (both over other men and over the instincts) is derived from control over external nature. This suggestion rests upon a confusion between the concepts of 'self' and 'society'. Domination as the category which mediates between the subject and nature is also referred at the very outset to society. The consequence of this approach is a reductive treatment of intersubjectivity. In compensation for this the categories of the 'subject' and of 'nature' must be applied in an inflationary way; they directly constitute the conceptual basis for a theory of cultural evolution which is reconstructed abstractly as *the history of the subject*. Thus at one point the attribute of subjectivity is imputed to the mythical activity by which an otherwise chaotic environment is bound together in a network of symbolic meanings, and at another point is ascribed to the purposive-rational activity by which nature is controlled through technology. But the abstractions employed by Horkheimer and Adorno – subject and nature – could only have the theoretical power of both holding together and differentiating between separate phases of world history if they were related to the primary dimension of intersubjectivity in which social life is organised. Only then would it be possible to produce a differentiated model of distinct kinds of social organisation, distinct social formations.

By reducing the dimension of intersubjectivity Horkheimer and Adorno lose two vital components of Marx's analysis: the notion of the self as *socially produced*, and the understanding of domination as referring to *variable kinds of social structure*. This both restricts the concept of the self and confuses the meaning of domination.

Dialectic of Enlightenment is post-Cartesian in the sense that the self is defined with reference to an outside; but the outside is subsumed under the category of nature, and the process of self-definition is viewed solely under its negative aspect of opposition, as control, subjugation, exploitation. This understanding of identity formation is deficient because no notion of the self is possible without a concept of intersubjectivity. Men decide who they are in terms of the outside social reality to which they are related in a basic way, both within the cellular family and in relation to larger communities. Even as children their still untamed instinctual desires encounter the rules of their society, as a set of explicit or implicit expectations. This is the reality to which they must adapt in order to survive, and in the beginning that adaptation is induced by external coercion. Then, as they grow up, social expectations become internalised; a conscience takes shape which requires the observation of social rules 'from within'. We acquire, as it were, internalised parents. This process of identity formation inevitably has a negative aspect. For it is impossible without renunciations. The environment in which children live permits them to express their immediate feelings without too much hindrance, and offers to do a lot for them in response to their often drastic demands for immediate gratification. They experience this condition for a long time before they grow to understand that it was made available to them only at the cost of others: only, as it were, parasitically. To observe the behaviour of a one-month-old child is sometimes to be put in mind of someone who finds himself in a first-class hotel, all services laid on. But equally, to observe the behaviour of an adult forces the recognition that the formation of identity is always susceptible to regression. Perhaps no one can do without the aid of some infantile adaptations. We are always tempted, especially under stress, to fall back on mechanisms of defence, the clichéd reactions of the child within us. Our ego is constantly prone to slip. Freud was right to draw attention to the co-existence of primitive modes of reaction and later stages of development. But to stress the continuing possibility of this regressive tendency is to perceive identity formation only in its negative aspect. Identity formation also receives a positive aspect from the intersubjective context which alone makes it possible. It contains both a dimension of freedom and a dimension of sharing. Neither is acknowledged in *Dialectic of Enlightenment*, yet they are reciprocally related. It is impossible to discover one's identity if one simply passively reflects the dominant meanings of the social world. To decide what kind of human being one is entails developing the capacity for critical insight, so that one can once more reconsider, and even partly redirect, the rules one has internalised. This judgement is an achievement of the ego, which must find authentic ways of expression by loosening its bonds to mere instinctual desire and social conformism. In this way the ego in the formation of identity has won a degree of freedom both inwards, in self-understanding, and outwards, in the judgement of social rules. It is also impossible to discover one's identity simply in a relation of rejection to outside social reality, for that is in part self-rejection. Any notion of private fulfilment which does not take account of its dependence on community is a contradiction in itself, because the discovery of authentic forms of self-expression is something one owes to some human community. The independent being can incorporate these forms in himself only through 'identification', that is, through attachment to others so that he can receive. And through this incorporation he can step beyond the inner problems of the self so that he is able to give because he is able to see himself as part of the larger community. In this way the capacity to share and the capacity to act as an independent being are reciprocally related; no notion of the self is possible without both elements; and so no concept of the self is possible without a concept of intersubjectivity.

Dialectic of Enlightenment is further vitiated by its diffuse understanding of domination. The central argument, that instrumental control over the environment is paid for by social control, rests on an unclarity in the concept of domination. For the question provoked by this thesis is: How in fact does domination over 'first' (external) nature turn into dominion over 'second' (social) nature? How does the unavoidability of social control result from the unavoidability of technical control? The answers to these questions as proposed by Horkheimer and Adorno are vulnerable to criticism since two dimensions of domination – control by men over nature, and control by men over other men – are not adequately separated. Because of this it is possible to cite propositions from *Dialectic of Enlightenment* in which the primary process is explained in two different ways. On the one hand, and in line with the main thrust of their argument, they claim that at the great turning points of western civilisation, 'whenever new nations and classes more firmly repressed myth', fear of uncomprehended and threatening natural forces was debunked as an animistic illusion, and 'the subjugation of nature was made the absolute purpose of life within and without'.[49] The development of discursive logic serves this goal; it enables men to distance themselves from nature so that they are able to form a concept of it for themselves – 'but only in order to determine how it is to be dominated'.[50] Instrumental tools and discursive concepts here have analogous functions. An instrumental tool which transforms nature is held on to in different situations as the same thing; because of this it divides the world into the chaotic, many-sided and disparate, on the one hand, and the known, one and identical, on the other. Discursive concepts exercise the same function in thought; they separate the disparate from the identical. 'The concept is the ideal tool, fit to do service for everything, wherever it can be applied.'[51] On the other hand, Horkheimer and Adorno sometimes seem to claim that discursive concepts do not so much serve directly the goal of subjugating nature as rather some particular social function. Thus, for instance, when a social order based on fixed property puts an end to nomadic existence, mastery and labour are divided; and at this point the development of discursive logic, which is 'domination in the conceptual sphere', is 'raised up on the basis' of actual social domination.[52] Here they appear to derive 'the dissolution of the magical heritage' from a change in the conditions of material production when they claim that it 'expresses the hierarchical constitution of life of those who are free'.[53] Even the 'deductive form of science' which supersedes the magical heritage by its demand for conceptual unity is said to contain categories of thought which have a 'social character', not because they are 'an expression of social solidarity', but because they 'reflect' hierarchy and coercion; the way in which scientific method seeks logical order by connecting concepts in a union of interdependence is 'grounded in the corresponding condition of social reality – that is, of the division of labour'.[54] Confusion here arises over the primary process because an attempt is being made to relate together two quite distinct historical transformations. There is the transition from myth to enlightenment, where pre-Socratic cosmologies may be said to mark the point of transition because they are rationalisations of the mythic mode of apprehension. And there is the transition from pre-capitalist communities to capitalist social formations, which is established by the institution of wage labour. But what is seen as the decisive break in history, the transition from myth to enlightenment, is never brought into clearly articulated connection to the specific break between pre-capitalist formations and capitalist formations. Because of this the critique of domination becomes dispersed; there is a lack of differentiation between the spheres of social life with which the concept of domination deals and insufficient clarity as to the precise causal weight to be given to different constituents of the social order. This highlights the decisive failure to reflect on the fact that any philosophy of history must always presuppose intersubjectivity.

The diffuse concept of domination has the same origin as the restrictive understanding of self-formation – the reductive treatment of intersubjectivity. This means that the argument advanced in *Dialectic of Enlightenment* stands in ironically impotent relation to the object of which it offers a critique. Horkheimer and Adorno are right to see that technological society, by treating nature merely as transformable matter, creates a man-made environment on an unprecedented scale from which the explicit ascription of meanings tends to be eliminated. And they are also right to claim that it generates an industrially produced publicity which creates a synthetic mutuality through the electronic transmission of messages. But what they do not stress is that technological society necessarily entails a process of privatisation.[55] The natural environment is transformed so radically that man becomes isolated from the natural environment and so from the shared communal meanings which belonging to such an environment entails; and the transformation is so all-pervasive that the capacity of partial societies within it to create a counter-community is severely curtailed. But the man-made environment is also largely devoid of obvious meaning; for it is the result of the drive for production of individuals and corporations, together with the striving by individuals to escape from the resulting environment. The result is the fragmentation of community. Because public meanings are eroded, there is a retreat into privatised meanings. The theoretical attempt to solve by private meanings the basic problems of existence, like the discovery of one's identity, goes hand in hand with the practical attempt to solve by private solutions the material problems of life, like living standards. This privatisation of life not only tends to dissipate the relation of giving-and-receiving in the actual community. It also makes it more difficult to perceive that all social formations, including those characteristic of a technologically developed society, must still, in principle, presuppose intersubjective rules. Yet precisely this blocking out of the intersubjective dimension is the basic weakness of *Dialectic of Enlightenment*. In that sense the critique which it presents is a further symptom of the disease which it seeks to diagnose.

5

Technological rationality

Marx's social ideal – the classless society – is not something which he posits as a moral imperative. For him, as for Hegel, an 'ideal', in the strict sense of the term, as something which is isolated or can be abstracted from the totality of the historical process, is a completely empty and meaningless concept. His philosophy of history, supported and elaborated by his studies in political economy, is intended to replace the moral appeal of the utopian socialists. For he was convinced that the objective conditions of capitalist society were driving towards the conclusion of a classless society. He can be said to have produced a critical theory of capitalism – rather than a utopian attack upon it – because his critique had an anchor: he analysed that social system from the point of view of the possible change in its basic structure. He thought that he could locate the possibility of change as it was already embodied, though latent, in pre-revolutionary conditions. Adopting a Hegelian coinage, he expressed this in the concept of the 'negative'. The 'negative' connotes those historical forces which are incompatible with a certain form of social life and act upon it destructively; but forces which nonetheless arise inevitably out of the particular social structure which they both negate and explode. And Marx believed that he had been able to locate this negative force at two points: in a mechanism, and in an agent.

Marx argued that the mechanism propelling the movement of history was the contradiction, at certain moments of development, between the forces of production and the relations of production. The forces of production are dependent on the level of scientific knowledge and technical equipment, and on the organisation of labour. The relations of production are manifested in property relations. In Marx's view, the bourgeoisie could maintain its ascendancy only by constantly creating more powerful methods of production. But the relations of production are not transformed at the same rate. Although the capitalist system produces more and more, poverty remains the lot of the majority. And it was this contradiction between the forces and the relations of production, Marx believed, that would eventually lead to a revolutionary crisis.

But the unprecedented increase in the forces of production has had the opposite effect from that anticipated by Marx. It has not been a historically explosive force in the way he had thought it would be. It has become a means of justifying the status quo. So history itself has turned on its head Marx's contention that the relationships of production – the power structure of society – could be measured, and found wanting, against the potential for development reached by the forces of production. For now the existing relations of production can be represented as that form of organisation which is technically necessary for a rational society; all problems can be made to seem to be questions of technical adjustment. This means that, once they have reached a very high level of development, the forces of production stand in a new relationship to the relations of production. Previously they offered grounds for a critique of the power structure of society; now they provide a basis for its legitimation.

The technology of advanced industrial society also makes possible the virtual elimination of those particular conflicts which Marx's diagnosis intended to bring to light, by assimilating into the social system the one class designated by him as the second 'negative' force within capitalist society: the proletariat. Marx saw that the working class which had been brought into existence through the process of capitalist production was no longer a class of society in the traditional sense; that is to say, it was not distinguished from other classes by the nature of its possessions. For it possessed nothing but its labour power and in order to secure a livelihood it had to sell this to those who owned the means of production. So the proletariat, as a class existing within a social order which rested on the principle of possession, was in fact the negation of that order. Once it had grown to an awareness of this fact – and it was of course the task of the Marxist philosopher to induce in the proletariat an awareness of its historical mission by bringing this negative fact to consciousness – then the proletariat would be able to draw the consequence from this self-knowledge. It would become the collective historical agent transforming the capitalist structure built on the principle of possession, because it was a class whose lack of possessions meant that its real needs could only be satisfied through the overthrow of that capitalist order. Marx believed, then, that the growth of revolutionary consciousness in the working class was necessitated by their place within the productive process, and by their being forced to an awareness of that place and of the concrete possibilities of action open to them.

But now, even if the critique of society can still be said to have a 'head', it seems to have lost its former 'heart'. Even though the majority of the population still do not have control over the means of production, the working class, as a proletariat, appears to have evaporated. In theory, the new skilled working class could disrupt, reorganise, and redirect the methods and relations of production. But they have neither the interest nor the vital need to do so. The social compensations they receive in the form of income, welfare securities, and education, are just sufficient to see to that. Indeed, the communications industry has so far structured their needs and aspirations that they often in fact turn into a counter-revolutionary force. It appears that affluence brings everyone to neighbouring levels of prosperity, with certain differences; the worker may be in a Mini and the director in a Rolls, but this difference is not large enough to carry with it any kind of really disruptive social dynamism. The proletariat have turned into the administered. They have on the whole relinquished pretensions to self-government, since they are more or less comfortably organised by others.

In his early writings Horkheimer followed Marx in believing that the proletariat was the agent through whose collective action the truth of his analysis would be confirmed; the critical theorist saw his activity as forming a unity with that of the oppressed class because his disclosure of social contradictions aimed to make a contribution towards the transformation of society.[1] Admittedly, the unity of critical theory and proletarian practice no longer works so smoothly for Horkheimer as it had for Marx. Marx had believed that philosophy would be transcended in the revolutionary action of the proletariat, whereas Horkheimer, faced with the collapse of the German working class movement, reclaims for critical theory a right to continued existence; the unity of critical theory and proletariat exists now only as a conflict;[2] and, in opposition to Marx and Engels, he no longer believes that the position of the proletariat within the productive process offers a guarantee of correct knowledge.[3] This pessimism, present at the outset, soon becomes more marked. Horkheimer and Adorno later noted, in passing as it were, the disappearance of a potentially revolutionary proletariat. That too was an achievement of instrumental reason which blunted the experience of need and scarcity, and hence their political articulation. Marcuse also admits that the working class 'has been dissolved *as a class*; the wish to build a qualitatively different social order has given way to the need for better conditions of work, more leisure time ... more material goods'.[4]

Marcuse acknowledges that in political systems generally regarded as democratic, as distinct from overtly fascist, capitalist societies provide certain conditions indispensable for the formation of a critical public. The principle of tolerance embodied in the political constitution is justified by the argument that no group or individual is capable of defining what is right and wrong, good and bad; competing opinions must therefore be submitted to the deliberations of the people. This democratic argument contains two implications. It implies the necessary condition that people must be capable of deliberating and choosing on the basis of knowledge, that they must have access to authentic information, and that, on this basis, the development of their society must be subject to the surveillance of autonomous critical thought. And it implies that improvements in the structure and values of the established society would come about in the normal course of events, prepared, defined, and tested in free and equal discussion, on the open market-place of ideas and goods. But, Marcuse claims, these theoretical claims do not square with reality. All kinds of covert decisions reached in negotiations between opposed interests have been made prior to their ostensible public discussion. These decisions come into force in such forms as the juxtaposition of gorgeous advertisements with unmitigated horrors, in the introduction and interruption of the broadcasting of facts by overwhelming commercials. This tolerance towards deception in merchandising and planned obsolescence, the manipulation of the banal and the terrifying, are no mere aberrations; they are necessary elements within a covertly repressive system which undercuts the possible formation of a critical public.[5]

The capitalist system is able to do this because it has developed to the point where the affluence which it generates makes it possible for the productive system to harness the libidinal energies of men to its own ends. Those who are constitutionally free are libidinally bound to the commodity-form in at least two senses. Individuals must learn to consume. Through the systematic inter-play between enticement and indulgence, they are satisfied by a profusion of ephemeral commodities the desire for which is con-stantly stimulated; the need to possess, consume, handle and constantly renew the gadgets, devices and instruments offered on the market becomes a biological need. And, together with this, permanent offers of diffused sexual gratification pour in from the outside world. Through the 'socialisation' of the body as a sexual object, it becomes desirable merchandise with high exchange value; by invading formerly private and protected spheres, the commodity-form is universalised. Thus in individuals themselves Marcuse sees at work a dynamic that *internally* negates possible liberation. They live in a society which is reproduced not only in the mind, in the concepts which men hold, but also in their senses. Once its values are firmly established as norms of social behaviour, they are not simply introjected – they also operate as norms of organic behaviour. The human organism receives certain stimuli and repels others in accordance with the introjected morality. Below the level of conscious ideology, capitalist society perpetuates patterns of behaviour and aspiration as part of the 'nature' of people; a gigantic apparatus of culturally created, but unnecessary, needs 'sinks down' into the biology of mankind.

How then is it still possible to urge the necessity of liberation from a relatively well-functioning and affluent society, where the demand for liberation is without a mass basis and therefore politi-cally impotent? Marcuse's position among the older representa-tives of critical theory is distinctive because he seeks to confront this problem. The third stage of critical theory sees a renewed search for the 'negative'.

A possible way out of the difficulty is to redefine the nature of the conflict which is latent but potentially explosive within the social structure. Since in an affluent society the economic motivation diagnosed by Marx no longer operates as an explosive force, the critique of society might shift its argument from the sphere of political economy to that of metapsychology. A critique which is no longer socially represented by any specific group or institutional sector might choose to shift the level at which it operates. This change of level is a logical result of a critique which, in *One-Dimensional Man* as in *Dialectic of Enlightenment*, sees its object not primarily as late capitalism but as 'technological rationality'. So in *Eros and Civilization* Marcuse offers a revision of Freudian psycho-analysis as a replacement for the now defective economic argument, and the concept of 'instinctual repression' here plays for Marcuse a role similar to that of 'economic exploitation' in Marx. The primary conflict is defined as taking place between technical rationality and latent human needs.

It is of course not the Freudian theory as a whole which is of interest to Marcuse, but only his later metapsychology, 'his reconstruction of the past history of mankind'.[6] In Freud's view the history of man is the history of his repression. Civilisation is based on the permanent subjugation of the instincts and their deflection to socially useful activities. This change is described by Freud as the transformation from the 'pleasure principle' to the 'reality principle'; men learn to give up immediate and uncertain satisfactions for the security of delayed and restrained pleasures. Marcuse revises Freud's diagnosis by arguing that the repressions so far characteristic of all human civilisations arise from the special conditions which have until now prevailed in the evolution of culture: the need to master nature in the struggle against scarcity. But if this is so, then the repressive organisation of instinctual life is due to factors which do not arise from the inherent nature of the instincts but from specific historical conditions to which the instincts have so far had to adapt. So the 'reality principle' is not universal. It is culturally specific to an economy of scarcity. But in a civilisation which tends to remove the obstacle of scarcity, repression is increasingly 'surplus repression'; repression in excess of that necessary for maintaining civilisation.

On this ground Marcuse suggests that instrumental reason, and hence a society whose guiding principle is technical efficiency, is potentially self-undermining. For technology has now reached a point where it can operate against the repressive use of energy insofar as it minimises the time spent in the production of the necessities of life, and so makes possible a substantial release of instinctual energy formerly bound up in toil and the domination of nature. There is no longer any inherent necessity, in terms of the struggle for existence, for civilisation to be repressive. The possibility of utopia is inherent in the technology of advanced industrial societies. This would involve a psycho-biological, as well as social and political, revolution. It envisages a 'psychic Thermidor'.[7] In this way Marcuse claims to validate his attempt to 'develop the political and sociological substance' of Freud's metapsychology, since psychological categories have become, on this interpretation, 'political categories'.[8]

Whether this is really so is a moot point. In *Eros and Civilization* Marcuse argues that the high level of instrumental rationality is the precondition for liberation. But in *One-Dimensional Man* he argues that it is this same development of the productive forces which is the effective basis for stifling potential rebellion or liberation. It comes as no surprise, then, that in *Das Ende der Utopie*, written in 1967, Marcuse admits that he is caught in a vicious circle. Today, he says, we face the problem that the transformation of society is objectively necessary, but that the need for this transformation is absent among precisely those strata who were classically designated as its agents. It is first of all necessary, therefore, to remove the mechanisms that stifle this need. But that, in its turn, presupposes the felt need for their removal. And that is a dilemma, he concedes, from which he has found no escape.[9]

The dilemma arises from the basic weakness in his diagnosis. The swing from hope to despair issues from a blurred vision of the distinctively political. He has not in fact succeeded, as he claims to have done, in transforming Freud's psychoanalytic categories into political categories. It is of course true that he seeks to demonstrate that his theory of change is compatible with certain aspects of psychoanalytic theory. But – and this is the crucial point – the possibility of change is not derived from psychoanalytic insights. It is dependent, rather, on Marcuse's technological determinism.

As one commentator has observed, Marcuse's hope and his despair are equally based on some assumption of a constant, predeterminate technological threshold that can in itself function to exclude or to impel the historical transformation for which he hopes.[10] So this historical threshold is seen, simultaneously, as both distant and near at hand. It is distant because manipulation is universal; the concept of 'one-dimensionality' assumes the existence of a system so internally consistent that it has the power of absorbing all practical intentions which might seek to subvert it. And yet the threshold is near at hand, because the system is described as one of 'technological rationality'; this is fragile because it is not firmly anchored, according to Marcuse's analysis, in the practical will of any group of men. On both sides of this paradox Marcuse underestimates the importance of practical intentions.

The paradox is manifest in two concepts which in Marcuse's writings have acquired the status of a fetish. These are the concepts of the 'apparatus' and its counterpart, the 'great refusal'.

The idea of an apparatus is Marcuse's favourite formula for the description of advanced capitalist society. It is true that he notes that science, by virtue of its neutrality, becomes susceptible and subject to the objectives which predominate in the society in which science develops, and that at present this is still a society in which the exploitation of natural resources takes place through the exploitation of man. However highly developed its technological potential may be, 'even the most highly organised capitalism retains the social need for private appropriation and distribution of profit as the regulator of the economy'.[11] This implies that in capitalist society, and in the socialist societies which are forced into competition with it, the development of technology is conditioned now, as before, by particular interests extrinsic to scientific methods themselves. Nonetheless, this line of thought is constantly being undercut in Marcuse's analysis by reference to an all-inclusive 'apparatus'. This idea he derives from the work of Weber. Weber had been the first to suggest that capitalism, far from perishing from its internal contradictions, becomes ever more solidified as the technical efficiency within the system of production extends to all spheres of society. The rationality found in the ethos of work, in industrial discipline, and in specialisation, are transferred from the sphere of economics to those of politics and administration. As the bureaucratic apparatus becomes ever more perfect, industrial society tends to bring the spirit of capitalism – calculating rationality – into synthesis with the logic of domination – social control. Marcuse not only accepts Weber's diagnosis; he even intensifies it. He sees the distinguishing feature of industrial society in its high level of technical rationality, and he focuses on the changes which arise from the process of its diffusion. This total control over men and things is seen as having arisen historically from the practice of capitalist appropriation; but in its present phase it is no longer possible to recognise the capitalist origins which lie behind the process of rationalisation. From this inter-pretation a view of rationality emerges in which bureaucracy and technology are seen as having become in themselves agencies of control. Economic exploitation tends to be superseded by abstract 'totalitarian' control. 'Technological rationality' is the central category. Under this heading, economic laws, political forces and technological developments are conflated into a single, undivided unity; to which of these priority within the system is to be ascribed can no longer be decided. Marcuse has thus renounced the attempt to give a systematic account of the way in which an interest which is constitutive for the stability of the industrial system seeks to maintain that stability; although he mentions the fact that there are antagonistic interests at work in society, he fails to show precisely how technological rationality may be derived from such antagonism. However difficult it may now be to localise this antagonism within the social structure, the refusal to undertake the attempt means that a historical dimension, on which critical theory is dependent, has been lost.

The abstract idea of the 'great refusal' forms the counterpart to the equally abstract idea of the 'apparatus'. It flows logically from the thesis of 'one-dimensionality'; for unless Marcuse is prepared to qualify his claim concerning the universality of manipulation by conceding the existence of structural gaps within the system of repressive rationality, the critical theorist has to forgo any attempt to explain the fact of his own existence. If the apparatus really blocks all possible change, then the vision of a liberated society becomes, for those who are able to conceive of it, a mysterious privilege: they are unable to say from which structural conflicts and interests they derive this conception. Even the appeal to consistent biological needs remains abstract so long as it is impossible to specify those areas or institutions within the structure of industrial societies, in which these needs can be felt and can exert a penetrative force *as social interests*. For biological needs cannot transform an institutional system directly, but only indirectly through their translation into changing intentions. This leaves Marcuse's critique in a stalemate position, since he fails to point to any group or class as the necessary and effective vehicle of the consciousness of the revolutionary possibilities which he believes to be inherent in the present historical stage of production. It is true that in *An Essay on Liberation* he claims that there is a minority which might rescue the majority from a condition in which they have been so far manipulated that they cannot perceive or express their true needs. He argues that the opposition in advanced societies is concentrated in the ghetto population and among students. But these two groups do not form the human basis of the social process of production, and they are often faced with hostility from among the ranks of organised labour. It has a 'preparatory function', but by itself, Marcuse concedes, the student movement is 'not a revolutionary force'.[12] And so it is not surprising when he subsequently suggests that the concept of revolution could in the foreseeable future become 'a merely abstract and speculative undertaking'.[13] For what he has shown to be possible is not organised political action, but only the production of symptoms expressive of the situation itself: what Lenin in his diagnosis of 'Left-Wing Communism, an Infantile Disorder', described as the 'petit-bourgeoisie, driven to frenzy by the horrors of capitalism'. Hence no clear programme of sustained political action could emerge from his analysis, but only the cult of the immediately rewarding gesture. There is one such gesture which Marcuse is fond of quoting. In the evening of the first day of the July Revolution of 1830, simultaneously but independently at several places, shots were fired at the clocks on the towers of Paris. This, Marcuse infers, reflects the conscious wish to 'break with the continuum of history' which marks the revolutionary class in the moment of action: an awareness of the 'totality of the rupture between the new society and the old'.[14] This story tells us as much about Marcuse as about the revolutionary class. It is characteristic that he should invite us to contemplate beguiling and spectacular emblems of change, which are made to stand as a substitute for a specific analytic account of the processes and dynamics of possible change.

Both his diagnosis and his prescription betray a curious atavism. The basic components of Marcuse's vision of technological domination were in fact founded on the over-simple identification of fascism, monopoly capitalism, totalitarianism and technology, a set of identifications first built up before the Second World War.[15] As early as 1934 Marcuse fell back on the concept of an 'apparatus' in his interpretation of fascism. In his essay on 'The Struggle Against Liberalism in the Totalitarian View of the State' he described fascism as 'an order which is maintained through the power of an enormous apparatus – an apparatus which can represent the whole over individuals because it represses them wholesale, forming a totality only by virtue of the total control of all'.[16] And when in his later writings he describes advanced industrial society as 'totalitarian', he identifies fascist and late capitalist society in aggressive simplification. Criteria which might make it possible to differentiate between specific features in the technically most advanced centres of the contemporary world are sacrificed to an appeal to decide against that world. The proposal of the principle of a 'definite choice', the 'great refusal', has a quasi-accidental and arbitrary quality. It is a decision. By limiting the focus to the here and now, this once again brackets out from his critical theory of society the problem of historical continuity; the standpoint of the existentialist 'choice' is reproduced anew. Ironically, this position has a curious affinity to that which he sharply criticised in the same essay of 1934. His theory of a 'definite choice' – which presupposes the total negation of the prevailing order – stands in striking parallel to the repressive tendencies of 'decisionism' which in 1934 he had not hesitated to describe as fascist.[17]

The problems which Marcuse's incoherence discloses is one of topology. It is this: is it possible to define a boundary, and if so what is the nature of that boundary, between technology and the political use of technology? The situation is complicated by the fact that technology has become both an instrument and a competitor of politics. On the one hand, science and technology have become important instruments of political action; on the other hand, they have developed a life of their own and so become a new source of authority and power in society, one with which those directly involved in political action have to reckon. But whether as an instrument or as a competitor they have the effect of devaluing the distinctively political.

6

Language and politics

Habermas sets out to unravel the incoherence which befogs Marcuse's analysis: is it possible to define a boundary, and if so, what is the nature of that boundary, between technology and the political use of technology? But this of course is part of a much larger enterprise, which involves at the outset two further refinements. Habermas seeks to modify the concept of critique as understood by the ostensible point of reference for critical theory, Marx, and as expounded by its original proponent, Horkheimer.

One aspect of historical materialism is problematic not so much empirically as methodologically. Marx argued that under the conditions of the capitalist process of production the values of the goods circulating on the market were erroneously thought to be the properties of these goods in themselves, so that they could no longer be clearly perceived as the expression of socially constituted relations between classes of producers. And he argued that the categories used by economists like Adam Smith and Ricardo reinforced this illusion, for they misinterpreted the transient institutions of a historically-specific productive process by ascribing to them attributes similar to those of natural laws which are independent of historical variability. Yet there is a sense in which Marx himself fell into the same mistake of which he accused his opponents. He tends to interpret the facts of the social world, which are in principle institutional facts, in language and categories which make them seem as if they were natural facts. It would be quite wrong to see this as a primary intention of historical materialism; but it would also be wrong to deny the existence of this tendency. It is not so much spelt out as rather present by way of suggestion. This is strongly reinforced by Marx's reference to the natural sciences as providing a model for his own studies in political economy; that is, a form of investigation which is concerned exclusively with natural facts. Marx claims to represent 'the economic law of motion of modern society' as a 'natural law'; and in order to demonstrate the scientific character of his analysis he repeatedly makes use of its possible analogy with the procedure of the natural sciences. In fact he never gives strong evidence of having revised the intention expressed in his early writings according to which the science of man was to form a unity with the natural sciences. 'Natural science,' he once said, 'will eventually subsume the science of man just as the science of man will subsume natural science: there will be a single science.'[1] This tendency in Marx's thought may be termed scientism.

Marx's scientism can be viewed as the expression of a methodical attempt to pursue the study of social processes with as high a degree of precision and testability as possible. But there is always the danger of this scientism becoming ontological; that is, institutional facts are referred to in categories which can make it seem as if they really are natural facts. Natural laws are not the products of men; but many social processes can be understood only when it is recognised that they are in part determined by those rules which constitute social institutions. Money, the exchange of commodities, and wage labour are institutions in this sense. When the institutional aspect is not sufficiently highlighted there is a tendency towards the 'mechanistic' exaggeration of the theory of base and superstructure; the consciousness of men is seen in terms of a one-sided determination by the conditions of production. The conditions of production – essential elements of which are the institutional conditions of money, the exchange of commodities, and wage labour – tend to take on the features of natural facts even in the eyes of their critics, who lose sight of the extent to which the objects of which they produce a critique are systems of rules constituted through a process of intersubjective communication. To the extent that Marx's scientism becomes ontological in this way, rather than being viewed simply as a methodical device, it has serious consequences for the way in which systems of institutional rules are regarded. Questions regarding the discussion of received systems of social rules and the possible working out of newly constituted rules come to be felt as something which is largely irrelevant to the development of the 'material substructure' of society. This may well contribute materially to the idea of an inexorable course of history – especially when it is believed there are good reasons for supposing that a particular social system is in a condition where those elements within the system which might cause its collapse are no longer accessible to any decisive human intervention informed by a discussion of the goals and methods of such intervention.

The problem contained in the original formulation of historical materialism reappears in a new guise in Horkheimer's critique of scientism. Natural science, no less than money, the exchange of commodities, and wage labour, is in one of its aspects a system of social rules. Horkheimer's failure to elaborate the implications of this fact makes his critique of traditional theory in general and logical positivism in particular seriously deficient. Horkheimer wants to distinguish between two things: between the procedures of the natural sciences as these are tacitly understood by its practitioners and explicitly analysed in the logic of science, and the role which natural science plays in the productive system. As he interprets it, theory for contemporary science is 'the sum-total of propositions about a subject, the propositions being so linked with each other that a few are basic and the rest derive from these. The smaller the number of primary principles in comparison with the derivations, the more perfect the theory.'[2] As elements of the theory, as components of the propositions and conclusions, there are ever fewer names of experimental objects and ever more numerous mathematical symbols. Hence 'in so far as this traditional conception of theory shows a tendency, it is towards a purely mathematical system of symbols'.[3] But, in reality, the development of science and technology is an element in the continuous development of the material foundation of society. The fact, for example, that in the seventeenth century men began to resolve the difficulties into which traditional astronomy had fallen, no longer by supplementary constructions, but by adopting the Copernican system in its place, was not due to the logical properties of the Copernican theory alone; if these properties were seen as advantages, this very fact points to the fundamental characteristics of social life at that time; if Copernicanism, which was hardly mentioned in the sixteenth century, now became a revolutionary force, that fact was part of the larger historical process in the social conditions of manufacture by which mechanistic thinking came to prevail.[4] But quite apart from particular examples of this kind, Horkheimer argues that there is a close link between theory construction in the natural sciences and its technical applications; and this in the quite explicit sense that 'the manipulation of physical nature and of specific social and economic mechanisms' both demand 'the amassing of a body of knowledge' of precisely such a kind as is supplied 'in an ordered set of hypotheses'.[5] On this view, traditional theory is defective to the extent that it fails to give any account of the ways in which the procedures of the natural sciences are embedded within the primary process of material production. If the structure and function of scientific theories is to be comprehended, it is necessary to reconstruct the role they play in this process. Horkheimer's claim that theoretical developments in the sciences are dependent on the state of the productive process as a whole may be viewed as a counterweight to the stress given to the purely logical factors involved in the reconstruction of scientific development. But his concentration of focus on socio-economic factors can be equally one-sided. He is far too unspecific about the precise ways in which the sub-system of the natural sciences is to be related to the general system of productive conditions; and he thereby runs the danger of simply reducing logical to sociological categories. In this sense he seems au fond to accept the basis/superstructure schema – that is, the causal and methodological priority of the basis.

The danger of reducing logical to sociological categories can only be avoided by unpacking the *a priori* assumptions of logical positivism more carefully than Horkheimer succeeds in doing. Thus it has to be assumed *a priori* in the logic of science not only that there exist facts which are independent of human thinking about them, but that those facts can be recognised intersubjectively as facts. In order to secure this intersubjective recognition the logic of science requires formalised languages. Such languages can formulate only facts, postulates, and logical inferences. As a matter of principle, these formalised languages cannot be used for intersubjective communication in the full sense of that word. That is to say, they cannot formulate utterances which involve personal identifiers, like I, you, we, – statements which directly express the situation of intersubjective communication and reflection on that situation. It is of course possible, in the logic of science, for utterances which involve personal identifiers to be the object of descriptions of verbal behaviour. But they can be the object of such descriptions only from a standpoint extrinsic to them; that is, such descriptions as may be used by an observer of a communication who in principle does not participate in that communication. A description of verbal behaviour in a formalised language cannot express an understanding of the intentions of the persons who are speaking, because to do this would imply that these persons and the describer participate in a common language game. But the language of science, as understood by the neopositivist logic of science, in principle excludes the existence of a language game which is common to the subjects and to the objects of science. It must exclude this. For the whole point of constructing formalised languages for scientific use is to eliminate problems of communication; that is, to eliminate the problem of interpreting one another's intentions, by establishing a framework of language which is *a priori* an intersubjective one.

But in order to construct such formalised languages science requires its own linguistic conventions. If one man alone could, at least in principle, practise science, then the conventions which are presupposed in the rational operations of scientific knowledge would have to be viewed as irrational personal decisions; a convention would be the same sort of thing as a solitary and arbitrary decision. But Wittgenstein demonstrated that one person alone cannot be said to follow a rule; thus he has shown that conventions presuppose language games. Applied to the philosophy of science, this means that the indispensable conventions about the meanings of concepts which are needed in scientific procedures presuppose that there are cognitive operations, such as the interpretation of signs, which rest on an exchange between men in a 'community of interpretation'. Only through the signs of a language are one scientist's intentions of expressing a meaning so connected with the possible intentions which another scientist may have of expressing meaning that either of them can really 'mean' something. In other words, 'I', as a natural scientist, have valid intentions of expressing meanings only because there exists a language in which not only 'my' meanings can be given fixed expression. This principle applies even in extreme cases, like the language of calculus, where the expression of a communicable meaning must take the form of what may be called a fixed 'sign-instrument'. Of course, when a formalised language is constructed out of such pure sign-instruments, the understanding of meaning depends only on participation in the conventional definition of the rules of a sign system. But even here, in the language game of calculus, the sign serves as the vehicle of the understanding of meaning; for its form is the fixed result of *a priori* understanding in a particular 'interpretation-community', to which the constructors and participants of the language of calculus must belong. Even here, therefore, cognition must presuppose interpretation of meanings – an exchange between men in a community of communication. The construction of a formal language is an indirect way of improving intersubjective communication for specifically delimited ends, and always presupposes intersubjective communication. This makes it possible to reformulate the critique of traditional theory. The critique would now state: natural science – that is, the description and explanation of objective events in space and time – presupposes interpretation in a communication community, because one man alone cannot follow a rule and thus cannot practise science. It follows that interpretation as a means of communication has a complementary function to description and explanation.[6]

This leads to Habermas' fundamental distinction between instrumental and communicative action.[7] In instrumental action we encounter objects the paradigms for which are moving bodies; in principle, these are capable of manipulation. In communicative action we encounter objects the paradigms for which are speaking and acting subjects; in principle, these can be understood through symbols. The contrast is between instrumental reason which is interested in the domination of nature, and comprehension which is interested in communication without the desire of domination.

As an example of instrumental action, we might cite Herman Kahn's predictions concerning the technical inventions which will almost certainly occur during the next thirty years. He predicts, for instance: new and more varied drugs for the control of fatigue, relaxation, alertness, mood, personality, perceptions, fantasies, and the improved ability to change sex. All these techniques refer to ways of controlling behaviour or of changing our personality which do not take effect by means of the indirect influence of social values through their internalisation by the individual; bypassing that process, they extend the direct manipulation of behaviour. The significance of that distinction is this: a value which I have internalised can effectively be apprehended by me, scrutinised, assimilated, resisted, reflected upon, in a way in which a drug which I have swallowed cannot be. This fact can be brought into closer focus if we consider it in the light of an example of what Habermas calls communicative action. One such example is suggested by Freud's decision early in his career to abandon hypnosis in favour of free association in the course of psychoanalytic therapy. The significance of that decision lies in this: hypnosis manipulates the processes of consciousness without handing them over to the full personal responsibility of the patient. It neither aims at nor succeeds in precipitating in him a sustained, and perhaps difficult, process of communication with another person together with a self-critical reflection upon his own behaviour. Whereas Freud believed that those memories of the patient which are recovered and fully grasped in the course of therapy by means of free association must lead to self-knowledge: that is to say, by means of a conscious re-appropriation by the patient of repressed pieces of his life-history. Habermas would say that since the intention of self-knowledge is built into the behaviour characteristic of psychoanalytic therapy, then this is an example of communicative action, and not of instrumental action.

I shall now run in parallel an abstract synoptic statement of what Habermas' distinction between instrumental and communicative action entails.

Men differ from animals because they manipulate the external natural world to a very much higher degree and in a more complex way. They make tools. Men also differ from animals because they communicate with each other to a very much higher degree and in a much more complex way. They speak and form concepts. These two types of activity are not a set of direct, instinctual responses; in both cases they are indirect or mediated. Actions of the first type are instrumental. Actions of the second type are symbolic. Instrumental behaviour is manipulative: it is the imposition of the human personality and human designs upon inert matter. Communicative behaviour is symbolic: it is the interaction between at least two people by means of signs.

The possibility of instrumental behaviour resides in the structure of the human organism. We have the possibility of bodily movement (through our arms and legs), the possibility of producing energy (through our body), the possibility of sensing external stimuli (through our eyes and ears), and the possibility of piloting or guiding the whole apparatus (through our brain). We supersede the enclosure of these capacities within our bodies by creating extensions of these capacities in the form of technical instruments and constructs. In the course of history the human race projects outwards into the form of such technical instruments and constructions all of these potentialities, one after the other, so relieving the human organism itself of the corresponding functions. This means that technological development in the course of history follows a logic: that of instrumental action.[8]

Analogously, the possibility of communicative behaviour resides in the structure of the human organism. We have the possibility of relating to others because we can look at them, touch them, talk to them. I supersede the enclosure of these capacities within myself by meeting with others in a network of relationships. The experience I have of my own identity is an experience of self-reflection: it is a relationship of the knowing subject with himself. But this self-awareness can never arise out of isolated self-reflection: it comes only through acts of reciprocity. I learn to see myself, in part at least, with the eyes of another person. So my self-awareness arises out of what may be called an intersection or complementarity of perspectives. Self-awareness can take shape only on the basis of some form of reciprocal acknowledgement: through acts of reciprocity alone can I become a self-reflective moral agent. So communication as it develops follows a logic throughout the course of human history which is distinct from that of instrumental action: it has of its essence the form of a dialogue.[9]

Instrumental and communicative action work according to two different types of rules. Instrumental behaviour obeys technical rules which rest on empirical knowledge. In every case these rules entail predictions about observable events, physical or social. These predictions, which may be correct or incorrect, tell us that under certain given conditions certain effects will follow. Communicative action, on the other hand, obeys social rules, which define reciprocal expectations of behaviour and must be understood and acknowledged by at least two people. Social rules are confirmed and strengthened by means of sanctions. The validity of technical rules depends on empirically or analytically correct propositions. The validity of social rules depends on a mutual understanding of intentions and can be guaranteed only by a general recognition of obligations. A violation of a technical rule we call incompetent behaviour. It infringes rules which have been tested in experiment and it is condemned *per se* to failure; the 'punishment' is, so to speak, built into the failure. A violation of a social rule we call deviant behaviour. It infringes rules that have been formalised by social institutions; and it provokes sanctions, or 'punishments', that are connected with the rules only externally, that is to say by convention. The crucial point about this distinction is that I cannot deviate from technical rules. If I break social norms this can be labelled deviant behaviour, which is punished by sanctions external to the norms. But if I break technical rules this is simply incompetent behaviour, which is sanctioned by the immediate failure of the intended strategy.

What Habermas wishes to say, then, is that the human race creates the structures of its historical life along two distinct – though always interrelated – dimensions. Instrumental action results in a technical achievement: it arises out of the attempt to free us from the external pressure of nature. Communicative action results in a self-reflective achievement: it arises out of the attempt to free us from the internalised pressure of obsolete legitimations.[10]

This distinction has both practical and theoretical consequences. The practical consequence is a sketch for a theory of politics. The theoretical consequence is a sketch for a theory of communicative competence.

Habermas' theory of politics aims to distinguish between social structures, according as to whether the mode of instrumental or communicative action predominates in them. He argues that advanced capitalism is best defined by the fact that its characteristic modes of action and language of explanation are drawn so substantially from the first sphere of action as to render increasingly inert the modes of behaviour and explanation typical of the second sphere of action. The upshot is to cause the distinction between 'technical' change and 'practical' change to become blurred and eventually to sink out of our awareness. Which is precisely why he wishes to bring that distinction to our attention again by differentiating between instrumental and communicative action. He is offering a counter-statement.

Habermas argues that advanced industrial society has brought into existence both a new type of social structure and a new way of justifying that structure. He locates the change from liberal to advanced capitalism in two movements.[11] The first is the increase of state intervention in economic life in order to shore up the stability of the system. The second is the growing interdependence of research and technology which has turned the sciences into the leading productive force. These two related changes have brought about a new constellation of forces which render Marx's terms of analysis increasingly obsolete; in Habermas' view, we can no longer understand how our society works by trying to produce a critique of political economy in the same form as Marx did. For when the separation of politics from economic life, characteristic of the liberal phase of capitalist development, is superseded by an increasing intersection of the two spheres, then the state and society no longer stand in the relationship of superstructure and infrastructure ascribed to them by Marx. But a method of analysis which seeks to understand the totality of society by first methodically isolating the laws of the economy could only claim to be able to grasp the essential structure of that society when politics were clearly dependent on an economic 'base'.[12] Now, however, the increase in state activities aims at eliminating dysfunctions that threaten the system. Indeed, it is in large part to these activities that the social structure owes its relative stability and capacity for adjustment: the function of the political system is chiefly that of circumspect 'crisis management' and long-term strategies for avoiding risks.[13] And this brings into existence a new concept of politics. The rules which guide administrative operations are 'technical-preventative' ones. In this new technocratic concept of politics the intention is not to carry into effect a just form of communal life but to preserve the smooth working of the social structure: hence it now appeals primarily to functional efficiency as the basis of its legitimation. Governmental activity is directed towards administratively soluble technical problems; and these problems are so framed as not to be properly a subject for public discussion – they must be handed over to the appropriate technical experts. This process is reinforced by the fusion of research, technology, production and administration into an interlocking system, in which the relationship between theory and practice comes increasingly to be understood in terms of the application of techniques based on empirical scientific knowledge: theory yields instructions for the manipulation of objective processes.[14]

Corresponding to this new mechanism, a new type of legitimation emerges. Habermas believes that Marcuse's thesis, according to which science and technology also take over the function of justifying the social order, provides the key for understanding the changed constellation of affairs. The liberal capitalist system had been justified by the notion of the 'just exchange' of commodities. Everything was referred to an impersonal common denominator; everything, as we say, has its price; or, as Marx once put it, a certain number of boxes of shoe polish are the equivalent of a palace. If an exchange of commodities was claimed to be just, that was because it was interpreted as an exchange of quantitative equivalences. But the concept of 'just exchange' was ambiguous. It looks, as it were, in two directions at once. The word 'exchange' refers to quantitative equivalences and speaks the language of functional rationality. Whereas the word 'just' refers to qualitative relationships and speaks the language of human reciprocity. The ideology of advanced capitalism tends to eliminate this ambiguity. Increasingly, society's self-understanding is detached from the frame of reference of communicative action and is expressed instead by a scientific model: that is, as a self-regulating system, in which the structure of instrumental action absorbs that of communicative action. This technocratic consciousness is, of course, like all the old ideologies in the sense that it hinders the fundamental structure of society from being clearly perceived. But in one important sense it is unlike them. For it is not, as they were, an illusion, a projection of the good life; it is not a collective wish-fulfilment or substitute gratification – nor a rationalisation in the Freudian sense of the term. And precisely for that reason it is less vulnerable to the attack of critical reflection. It is an ideology which does not embody a split between a moral sphere and some other sphere. It aims at the repression of the explicitly moral sphere as such. It makes the interest in free communication disappear behind the interest in technical control. The core of its false consciousness is that it obscures the distinction between instrumental and communicative action. By doing that, Habermas argues, it violates a practical interest grounded in one of the two fundamental conditions of our cultural existence: in language.[15]

In effect Habermas wants to restore a concept of the political which is indebted to the Greek polis.[16] In the polis, the slave class were subject to the necessity of labour, thus freeing the citizens for political discussion; in contemporary society the place of the slaves could presumably be taken by automation. But Habermas argues that a scientific–technical society could be rational only if the development and application of science and technology were subject to public control; and only if the autonomy and responsibility of workers were secured so that there was a framework of discussion free from domination. He feels the goal must be worked for by establishing a dialogue between men about the ends of life – although the institutional mechanics of this proposed dialogue remain unspecific. Thus, unlike Horkheimer and Adorno, he believes that practical reason could be a characteristic of society, not only of separate individuals. And unlike Marcuse, he sees the content of utopia as the creation of an ideal situation of public discussion in which communicative distortions are eliminated.

The theoretical consequence of this is the sketch for a theory of communicative competence.[17] This is reached by first considering forms of distorted communication.[18] In pursuing this line of investigation Habermas draws upon the hermeneutic method, that tradition of philosophical reflection on the rules for the interpretation of literary texts which reaches back in the Western tradition to Aristotle.[19] The central rule of this method is contained in the idea of the 'hermeneutic circle'. The idea is quite simply this: the interpreter of a text must seek to understand the particular in the light of the whole and the whole in the light of the particular; the text becomes intelligible through a scrutiny of all the individual words of which it is composed and of the way in which they are connected together; and yet the full understanding of the individual parts of the text already presupposes some prior or anticipatory comprehension of the whole. Each act of interpretation moves within this hermeneutic circle. Those whose concern has been with the interpretation of texts conceived along these lines have always of course been accustomed to meet obstacles to comprehension in the form of distortions and omissions in the texts; but these distortions and omissions were accidental. The interpretive method proposed by Freud, however, may be viewed as the invention of a new type of hermeneutics.[20] This was the study of texts, of which the dream is the paradigm, in which messages are systematically distorted; and one of Freud's finest achievements was his disclosure of the particular mechanisms which operated towards this end in dream-work – for instance, the processes of condensation and displacement. In this case, the distortions and omissions are put there by the author of the text intentionally, so that his own product becomes unintelligible to him. As a defence against unwished-for instinctual drives his intentions are rendered unconscious through a censor; the activity of the censor withdraws the interpretation of these instinctual drives from the experience of the subject. These intentions are in principle susceptible to interpretation, but only by decoding the systematically distorted form in which they have become expressed. It is the aim of psychoanalytic investigation to break down the distortions erected by the censor, and in this way to reconstruct the hidden connection of the symbols by means of which the subject deceives himself about himself. Dreams are the paradigm for texts which document the latent content of the author's intentions that have 'become inaccessible to him and alienated from him and yet belong to him nevertheless'.[21] Psychoanalysis may therefore be viewed as a kind of linguistic analysis which deals with systematically distorted communications.

But to view it in this way necessarily presupposes a theory of communicative competence.[22] Habermas' sketch for this starts from the idea of a smoothly functioning language game which rests on a background consensus. He argues that this consensus is based on the tacit mutual recognition of at least four types of validity claims which are implied in all speech acts. These claims are: that the utterance is intelligible; that its propositional content is true; that the speaker is sincere in uttering it; and that it is appropriate for him to be performing that particular speech act. In normal communication these claims remain implicit. But it is possible for situations to arise in which one or more of these claims becomes problematic in a fundamental way; that is, they cannot be dealt with simply by requesting more information or by clearing up misunderstandings within the accepted framework of opinions and values. When the background consensus is called into question in this way, specific methods are needed for resolving the problem. The claims, previously only implicit, now require discursive justification.

This leads Habermas to distinguish between communicative action and discourse. Discourse represents a definite break with the normal context of action. For ideally it entails two new conditions. It requires the putting out of play of all motives except that of a willingness to come to an understanding; and it requires a willingness to suspend judgement as to the existence of certain states of affairs and as to the rightness of certain values. Such discourses, Habermas argues, involve the supposition by the participants that they are in an 'ideal speech situation': the supposition, that is, that they are discussing under conditions which guarantee that the consensus which is arrived at will be the result of the force of the better argument and not of constraints on discussion. Habermas seeks to characterise this absence of constraint formally: the structure of communication can be said to be free from constraint only when for all participants there is an effective equality of chances to take part in the dialogue. Hence the requirements of the 'ideal speech situation' are such that the conditions for ideal discourse are connected with conditions for an ideal form of social life.

This is the link between the theory of communicative competence and the theory of politics. Habermas believes that the anticipation of a form of social life in which autonomy and responsibility are possible are prefigured in the structure of speech itself. Hence he views the theoretical and the practical consequences of his distinction between instrumental and communicative action as inextricably connected. His claim therefore is that the normative basis of critical theory is not an arbitrary one, but that it is inherent in the structure of social action which it analyses. In this way his theory of communicative competence may be seen to take the place of the analysis of the work process, once Marx's philosophical anthropology has been abandoned.

However, there is a crucial difficulty in this argument. It occurs at the point where Habermas takes psychoanalysis as the model for explaining the emancipatory effect of critical theory. In psycho-analysis, as I have said, the speech and actions of the patient are viewed as a system of symbols whose meaning must be reconstructed; the problem is to reconstitute a coherent meaning which has become unintelligible to the author of the text himself. This it seeks to accomplish by leading the patient, through a process of self-reflection, to become conscious of needs and motives that were previously repressed, so that he comes to acknowledge that these needs and motives are in fact his own. Habermas contends that this model can be, and should be, applied to society as a whole. The role of the critical theorist is to render those to whom he speaks autonomous by enabling them to comprehend their own situation in the social world.

But this transfer of the psychoanalytic model to large groups is more problematic than Habermas admits. In psychoanalysis, the patient's suffering and his desire to be cured provide the basis for the activity of the doctor who helps the patient to free himself from the compulsions which hold sway over him. This therapeutic relationship presupposes a voluntary subordination of one of the partners to the other; it also presupposes that both parties are committed to the liberation from affective constraints. For the analyst, the patient is not an object of manipulation, but a subject who is to be assisted to emancipation. It is of course true that the patient offers resistance to this process. But it is precisely by taking that resistance as a clue that the analyst seeks to lead him back to the original source of his anxiety. What the patient realises, as he begins to overcome his inner resistances, is that the occasions which repetitively give rise to his symptomatic behaviour do not exert over him a constraint which is strictly comparable to a natural force. He realises, on the contrary, that he contributes unconsciously to maintaining the condition of constraint from which he wishes to free himself. The aim of the therapeutic process is to bring the patient to see how he himself has reinforced his own state of servitude. Hence psychoanalytic therapy is neither a pure dialogue nor a process of external influence. It is rather a form of social interaction in which the assertion of one of the partners in the conversation (the doctor) concerning the inability of the other (the patient) to conduct a genuine dialogue, is finally recouped at the end of this process. Previously, agreement was not possible in the conversation concerning the assertion: 'You are incapable of dialogue.' Subsequently, agreement becomes possible concerning the assertion: 'You were incapable of dialogue.' As the patient gradually sets aside the previous restrictions on his capacity to communicate, he recognises that in the course of therapy it was necessary for the doctor to question his statements for what might lie 'behind' them, and hence to infringe rules of communicative action. Thus at the end of a successful therapy the patient acknowledges the legitimacy of two things: the non-communicative behaviour of the doctor; and the doctor's previous assumption that the patient was incapable of genuine dialogue. This is acknowledged by a patient who has been educated to be capable of dialogue; and the end result is possible only because of the common purpose uniting the doctor and the patient.

But precisely this common purpose is absent in social conflicts. In therapy, the aim of the doctor is to help the patient to free himself from his own resistances which impede the attempt he makes to free himself from internalised constraints. Whereas what obtains in a situation of social conflict is quite the reverse: here there is a condition of reciprocal resistance. For any ruling class the attempt to gain freedom from a social condition of compulsion must appear as a threat to the rule which it exercises over the other classes. And the oppressed class, for its part, will doubt the capacity of the dominant class to enter into a genuine discussion; and they will have good reasons for assuming that any attempts they make to enter into a dialogue with the ruling class may covertly be turned by the latter into an opportunity for strengthening the security of their rule; that the ruling class will resort to all sorts of manoeuvres for withdrawing any enforced concessions; and that in general their whole strategy will be based on an attempt to win back the terrain for which the revolutionary class have struggled. Hence the attempt to apply the psychoanalytic model to explain the practical effect of a critical theory of society founders upon this fundamental objection: the fact that the existing institutional structures and the control exercised through them by one part of society over the other are specifically designed to prevent the possibility that men might be able to reach an agreement which is not externally imposed but is based on a genuine dialogue about the right form of social life. To view a revolutionary struggle as a psychological treatment on a large scale is simply to obscure these brute facts of practical reality.

Given this essential difference between the condition of the psychoanalytic patient and that of any potentially revolutionary class, it follows that if the claim for emancipation is to be taken seriously only one way out of the difficulty remains: that is to say, a sustained attempt would have to be made, most probably against the will and perception of the dominant class, to break the institutional structures on which their authority rests. But Habermas has devoted comparatively little attention to investigating the sociology of institutions; and indeed the whole trend of his analysis deflects attention away from that area of the problem. Hence in a characteristic passage he says that 'when theory was still related to praxis in a genuine sense, it conceived of society as a system of action by human beings, who communicate through speech and thus must realise social intercourse within the context of conscious communication';[23] but that now 'socially effective theory is no longer directed towards the consciousness of human beings who . . . discuss matters with each other, but to the behaviour of human beings who manipulate'[24] by instrumental action. Hence 'no attempt at all is made to attain a rational consensus on the part of citizens concerning the practical control of their destiny';[25] for in contemporary society rationality is understood as something directed by technical control, 'but not by a coherent total consciousness – not by precisely that interested reason which can only attain practical power through the minds of politically enlightened citizens'.[26]

What practical power might mean in this context remains unexplained. But what is clear from the terms of his analysis is that the thrust of the argument is directed not so much at the lack of control over the productive process, but rather at the deficient consciousness or reflectiveness concerning that process. No doubt Habermas is right to see the dangers inherent in a society which is so far rationalised that it is able to deploy a vast, accumulated body of technical knowledge in the service of social domination; but 'consciousness' and 'reflection' alone are hardly sufficient to control that danger. What he opposes to technology in order to recover some degree of political control is the free communication of citizens. 'The basis of enlightenment', he says, is a form of knowledge 'tied to the principle of discussion free from domination, and solely to this principle'.[27] But all the concepts which he employs in order to characterise this countervailing force, notions like 'emancipation', 'responsibility' and 'autonomy', betray their historically-rooted origins in the pre-revolutionary period of the eighteenth-century Enlightenment. When he states that neither the political system of state-regulated capitalism nor that of bureaucratic socialism 'would stand up to the test of justification through discourse'[28] we may agree with him, but only because of the political triviality of the assertion. For to call the political reality of the present capitalist and socialist worlds before the tribunal of discourse is simply to bring the Judgement-Seat of Reason up to date: it repeats a bourgeois, pre-revolutionary abstraction. This dualism of reason and domination did indeed have a reality when it was first directed, in the eighteenth century, against the system of absolutism; at that time it referred to the concrete possibility of real, revolutionary events. But the dualism is no longer so apposite. Habermas' essays are exercises in a mode of thought whose basis lies in a historical period the politics of which can no longer be our own; so that, despite his strenuous efforts to re-establish their topicality, they are politically defective in the current social context. The insights of Historical Materialism are finally taken back into the pre-revolutionary concept of critical enlightenment.

Thus Habermas has failed to extricate himself fully from the incoherence in Marcuse's analysis. The problem which was expressed but at the same time confused in that analysis was, as I have suggested, the following: is it possible to define a boundary, and if so what is the nature of that boundary, between technology and the political use of technology? Habermas sought to solve the problem by avoiding the conflations contained within Marcuse's concept of technological rationality. It was for this purpose that he introduced his basic dichotomy between instrumental and communicative action. But that move itself leads to a further depoliticisation of critical theory. This begins already with the categorical separation of 'technology' and 'praxis'; the path is thus opened up for the reduction of 'praxis' to communication; and finally to the construct of the 'ideal speech situation'. The decisive move towards depoliticisation is inherent in the initial dichotomy: in taking as the point of departure the distinction between instrumental and communicative action.

7

Critique of critical theory

When critical theory is measured against the claims it makes for itself as a general procedure of social investigation, serious doubts arise. By explicitly taking Marx's *Critique of Political Economy* as the paradigm for their analysis of the contemporary situation, critical theorists open themselves to the question as to whether, in fact, they have succeeded in constructing a theory for their own society comparable in coherence and explanatory force with that produced by Marx for his society. Marx, as I have suggested, may be said to have produced an analysis of liberal capitalism that was critical in the sense that he analysed that system of production from the standpoint of the possible change inherent in its basic structure; he sought to locate the objective possibilities of change as they were already present, though latent, in pre-revolutionary conditions. But the analyses of the technically most advanced areas of the contemporary world produced by the main exponents of critical theory do not suffice to justify the claim that they have constructed a modern critical theory in this strong sense of the term critical. It is true of course that in shifting attention from the infrastructure to the superstructure they successfully highlighted the emergence of new dimensions of domination. But once they replaced the critique of political economy with that of instrumental rationality, they began to develop variants of an analysis which, although containing within them insights many of which were correct, or at the very least suggestive, did not amount, when they were viewed as a general frame of reference, to a fully coherent model that could be called critical in the sense in which that term can, quite justifiably, be applied to Marx's analysis.

In the writings of Horkheimer, Adorno, Marcuse and Habermas the attempt to reconstruct a coherent critical model constantly breaks down. It is not necessary to advert to subsequent history to show this; an immanent criticism of the theories themselves is enough to demonstrate the fact. We may perhaps choose to attribute these failures to faulty reasoning on the part of individual exponents of the tradition. But we can also see at work, or so I believe, two theoretical factors of a more general nature which help to explain the repeated breakdown of these 'critical' models.

The one is to be found in the connection between the ideas of critique and a particular philosophy of history. The other derives from certain unique features characteristic of the German sociological response to the onset of capitalist industrialisation. These two broad currents, in entering the tradition of critical theory, have interlocked and reinforced each other.

Let us turn, first of all, to the implication of critique. A range of meanings contained within the idea coalesced around a particular vision. The vision first crystallised in the last quarter of the eighteenth century when the theology of history was superseded by the German philosophy of history. This entailed more than the elaboration of an anti-theological argument. Before the end of the eighteenth century histories existed only in the plural; they were conceivable only as related to specific subjects. The term 'history' referred primarily to an occurrence or incident or a sequence of actions performed and endured; and it referred, secondarily, to information about these, an investigation and narration of them. Histories were always histories of a particular subject: the history of Charlemagne, of France, of the Church, of dogma. But in the last quarter of the eighteenth century 'history' as a plural form assumed the form of a collective singular.[1] It was now possible to formulate the previously inexpressible thought: 'History in itself'. History as a collective singular contained within itself the condition of the possibility of all individual histories. History, in this sense, came to occupy a position in the conceptual universe of the German language-area similar to that occupied by the concept of Revolution in France.

The formation of the concept of History as a collective singular does not of itself answer the question as to whether there is a point of reference which gives the events a unity. On the contrary, it provokes that question in the sharpest possible form: what, then, within History forms the basis of its unity? An answer to this question was found in the idea of Humanity, the Human Species.

Humanity is seen as possessing the unity of a subject, so that all the particular events in history might be imputed to Humanity as moments in the process of its self-realisation. If History is thought of as this process of self-realisation, then the subject which 'realises itself' must be presupposed. It is necessary to conceive of this Humanity which realises itself in the course of history naturalistically, if – dependent as it is on its resources alone – it is to be the subject which produces history. At this point the role of the subject of History, previously occupied by God, was imputed to Mankind; and the history of Humanity was now interpreted as a single project executed by this single agent.

It might be objected that the idea of Mankind as a collective subject is merely the projection on to a fictive entity of a real subjectivity which is found only in the human individual. The point was made by Marx in his attack on the Young Hegelians. Their interpretation of the 'world-historical collaboration of individuals' as the 'self-production of the species' which 'accomplishes the mystery of producing itself', is disposed of by him as 'speculative idealism'.[2] And the supposed autonomous existence of the 'class-as-individual', as distinct from the individual person, is criticised as one more expression of the condition of alienation caused by the division of labour.[3] Yet he himself frequently spoke of world history as 'the production of Mankind through human labour' – that is, as a process of 'self-production'[4] – and this still seemed to imply that hypostatisation of 'man', or rather of the human species, as the subject of History for which he had castigated the Young Hegelians. However that might be, the idea of a subject of history reappears in a different form with the argument that the emergence of capitalism has produced in the proletariat an agent by whom its own 'negativity' – analysed in the early writings as self-alienation and in the later writings as surplus-value – can be surpassed.

Horkheimer, Marcuse, Adorno and Habermas all reject important elements in the German philosophy of history. They no longer believe, with Marx, that the truth of their theory will be confirmed primarily in the historical action of the proletariat. And they no longer believe, with Hegel, that progress, however that might be defined, is guaranteed by a logic of history. Yet they are reluctant to abandon their roots in the myth of enlightenment – the view of history as one all-embracing process in which a historical subject attains its essence.

Thus the faculties originally ascribed by Kant to the consciousness of the transcendental subject are transferred by the early
Horkheimer to the human species. On this interpretation, Kant's
Critique had sketched out, albeit unknowingly and therefore in a
distorted form, the project of a future society which would become
truly productive.[5] Located now in a possible future, this rational
society, the goal of which is claimed to be 'really invested in every
man',[6] would be able to achieve concretely what Kant's transcendental subject could accomplish only formally: to transform chaos
into rational order. To seek this is to strive for a state of affairs 'in
which an all-embracing subject, namely self-aware mankind,
exists';[7] in the transition to the future form of society 'mankind will
for the first time be a conscious subject and actively determine its
own way of life'.[8] Yet the allegiance to the Enlightenment is
compromised by a penchant for Schopenhauer. This reinforces an
inclination to historical pessimism which is so insistent, even in his
early essays, as to cause him to suggest that the world is already
moving towards a condition comparable with the collapse of Antiquity.[9] It is true that this incipient gloom is always accompanied
by a rider: there is indeed, he claims, a general human interest in
the cancellation of social injustice; but, again under the influence of
Schopenhauer, he endows this interest with a voluntaristic
accent.[10] In fact he is so emphatic in stressing the necessity of a
partisanship for liberation that we begin in the end to suspect that
he does not entirely trust the emancipatory interest of Reason: a
suspicion corroborated when we find him conceding that no
indubitable proof can be produced for the existence of such an
interest.[11]

In Marcuse the Enlightenment heritage takes the form of what
has been aptly called a bifocal vision of history.[12] It is bifocal in the
sense that all realms of experience are bounded by two dimensions.
The first dimension is the established order, whether political,
economic, or sexual. The second dimension represents the aims of
men. This second dimension is embodied practically, in attempts
to alter that order; intellectually, in concepts which transcend the
facts imposed by that order; and passively, in the desires and
longings which are frustrated or rendered quiescent by it. All the
concepts of critical theory 'extend, as it were, between these two
dimensions, the first of which is the complex of given social relationships, and the second, the complex of elements inherent in the
social reality that make for its transformation into a free social

order'.[13] But Marcuse is unable to point to any particular class or group as the necessary and effective vehicle of the consciousness of the revolutionary possibilities inherent in the present historical stage of production. Thus his philosophy of history and its practical intention fall asunder, and a voluntaristic accent reappears to bridge the gap. It is called the 'great refusal', and it expresses the wish 'to break the continuum of history'.[14] But to introduce this concept is to concede the inability to connect the two poles between which critical theory is said to extend. The great refusal is identical neither with the right to resistance against political authority which was found in the theory of natural law, nor with the idea of emancipation which was expressed in Historical Materialism. For the subject of the refusal is not any fictively generalised historical subject which is represented by a corporate entity – a legislative body or a class within the system of production. It is the empirical individual, and his refusal takes place in the face of an anonymous system which exercises direct power over him.

If in Horkheimer and Marcuse the Enlightenment philosophy of history collapses back into voluntarism, in Adorno and Habermas it is subjected to a more systematic rejection – but a rejection which is never completed.

Adorno taboos the Hegelian belief that the course of world history may be viewed as forming an intelligible whole. Three events are cited in defence of this rejection: the miscarriage of revolution in Russia, the failure of revolution in the West, and Auschwitz. By the same token the 'atheistic Hegelians, Marx and Engels' are reproached for having produced an 'apotheosis of history'.[15] What Adorno objects to, in Marx and Engels as in Hegel, is the view which sees all that is negative in history as merely a necessary point of passage on Mankind's route through a historical process whose positive outcome is immanent. What he rejects is 'salvation history. That was the prototype of the concept of progress until Hegel and Marx.'[16] But, it may be asked, is there any qualitative difference between the negative, as it appears in capitalist exploitation, and the negative, as it appears in Auschwitz. Adorno would reply that there is: in Auschwitz we are confronted by a negative so radically evil that it cannot be dialectically surpassed. The experience of Auschwitz is here projected out of a specific historical conjuncture on to a view of history as a whole; it is viewed as the culmination of a process of civilisation which drives towards unlimited domination over nature. Adorno is so transfixed by this vision that he breaks his own taboo: he has rejected the idea that history forms a totality, and he then smuggles it back in. 'No universal history leads from Savagery to Humanity, but certainly there is one leading from the stone catapult to the megabomb.'[17] What was criticised in Marx as an apotheosis of history is transformed by Adorno into a 'diabolisation' of history. What was condemned in Hegel is once more turned on its head: radical evil – Evil as such – is promoted to the status of the World-Spirit. The history of salvation is replaced by the history of damnation.[18]

Habermas continues the work of demolition in a more sober spirit. He does this by proposing a sociological explanation for the philosophy of history. This he sees as an attempt to solve the problem of identity which was posed by the process of capitalist modernisation.[19] Specifically, he singles out two elements in the philosophy of history: the concept of progress, and the concept of self-emancipation through critique. Each of these he ties to a sociological base. In the first place, the capitalist mode of production provided a self-propelling mechanism which ensured long-term economic growth. The essence of capitalism is that scientific–technical innovation was institutionalised;[20] hence the experience of accelerated and directed social change, of accumulative economic growth, and of growth in technical control over the forces of nature. It is this experience that provided the basis for the idea of progress. In the second place, the success of the capitalist form of production detached the economic system from the political system. This made possible the exercise of systematic critical reflection released from the constraints of cultural traditions. Inherited political ethics began to yield ground to the claims of a universal morality, of which natural law theory was one of the most notable forms. In the long run, the executive power of the state could not remain immune from the claims of this new universal morality; for universalism, once extended to the sphere of political authority, required that all relationships of authority be justified on rational grounds. The experience of this contradiction between universal principles of justification and the particularities of political authorities provided the basis for the concept of historical freedom as self-emancipation through critique. On this interpretation, therefore, all universal histories of the human species were reflections of a particular historical experience: the process of capitalist modernisation within the framework of the nation-state.

By this procedure of sociological reduction, Habermas rejects as fictitious the idea of a 'human species which constitutes itself as the subject of world history'.[21] Yet Habermas also looks two ways; he is not prepared to complete the process of demolition. Thus he speaks of the 'achievements of the transcendental subject' as having 'their basis in the natural history of the human species';[22] and he frequently claims that there is a group which has an interest – he sometimes refers to this as a deep-seated anthropological interest – in emancipation. This subject is the human species; for Habermas too the subject of history, in the last resort, is Mankind. So in his Frankfurt Inaugural lecture of 1965 he speaks of the 'Idea' which is 'not mere fancy' but 'can be apprehended *a priori*'.[23] What raises the human species out of nature is language; 'through its structure, autonomy is posited for us'.[24] This 'autonomy posited with the structure of language' would only be fully realised in an 'emancipated society' where 'communication would have developed into the dialogue of all with all free of domination';[25] and the task of philosophy is to 'further the process' which constitutes 'mankind's evolution towards autonomy'.[26] These propositions clearly presuppose a teleological philosophy of history. Habermas cannot of course believe that the necessity of this teleology is guaranteed by divine providence. But that does not mean that within this concept of history no necessity is any longer conceivable. The assumption that there is a goal presupposes proof of the fact that the human species is necessarily able at least to approach it if not able to realise it fully. And so later Habermas continues to claim, in a way which re-echoes Horkheimer's interpretation of Kant, that what found distorted expression in the fiction of a 'self-producing subject of history' was the intention – to whom precisely that intention is to be imputed remains obscure – of controlling the development of societies by institutionalised and politically effective public discussions.[27]

Horkheimer, Marcuse, Adorno and Habermas all present variations on a single theme. Will they retain the Enlightenment philosophy of history or will they relinquish it? Their responses are always equivocal. They offer one answer with the right hand and another with the left. But this persistent prevarication is not simply the quirk of a group. It is a comment on the Enlightenment as well as upon critical theory. To understand this we must return once again to the moment at which the concept of Enlightenment received its classic expression.

It was in 1784 that Kant defined enlightenment as Mankind's departure from a condition of servitude which arose from its own fault.[28] Enlightenment is the attainment of human autonomy. To the extent that reason influences the shaping of human life, human history as a whole receives a direction and an assured progress. Thus Kant answered the question 'What is Enlightenment?' not metaphysically but in terms of a philosophy of history; and he defined the historical place of his own philosophy by viewing the age in which he lived as a whole as an age of enlightenment. Not the single individual but the whole epoch is freeing itself from the chains of the past. If enlightenment is to be achieved, it must be achieved in all spheres of life. In religion, it means the struggle for tolerance against superstition and the revolt of reason against the orthodox priesthood; in politics, the struggle for freedom before the law against the arbitrary despotism of estates; in natural science, empiricism; in philosophy, the liberation from the tutelage of theology and the fight against dogmatism and metaphysics. Enlightenment is not a private achievement but a general historical achievement. It is by definition universal: it embraces religion, politics, natural science, philosophy. If it is universal, it must entail the creation of a world for which man himself bears responsibility. A man who is autonomous has come of age; he claims to exercise his full powers; he can prove his autonomy only by taking full responsibility for his actions and their consequences.

It was the task of the philosophy of history to elaborate this claim to autonomy: to demonstrate that it is man himself who makes his world. All that appears to be imposed upon him from outside, all that seems to befall him by force of circumstance, he must learn to recognise as his own deed. It may indeed appear to him that the world is a datum, the operation of a kind of fate or destiny; but if that is so, then this is simply because he has forgotten that it is he himself who has made it. Here is born that theory of the unconscious which is to be found with varying nuances in Schelling and Hegel, in Marx and Freud.[29]

But the claim to autonomy bears the irremovable traces of the heritage which it seeks to disown. This is a theological heritage, and it foundered on the problem of evil. It was in 1710 that Leibniz first applied to this the term theodicy; theodicy, Kant was later to explain, is 'the methodical justification in a lawsuit, in which the divine management and government of the world is justified'.[30]

Thus the problem of evil is discussed in the language of a lawsuit. The subject of this lawsuit before the Judgement-Seat of Reason were the accusations brought against God's goodness and wisdom in view of all that is futile and evil in the world. Until the middle of the eighteenth century God was declared innocent of the charges levelled against him. Then, in 1753, the Prussian Academy of Sciences proposed, as the subject of a prize-essay, that the arguments in this debate be examined anew. At first, Kant was inclined to present again the arguments for the defence. But ten years later he had had second thoughts. In 1763 he placed the weight of his arguments on the side of the prosecution, and a little later he developed the theory of antinomies. On this view the world is full of unavoidable contradictions. But this incriminated the Creator of the world. God could now be pronounced innocent only if it could be shown that it was not God who was responsible for the evil in the world, for it was not He who makes and rules it but another. This other was man. The attempt to demonstrate this was the essence of Idealism. The effect of the demonstration was to bring the problem of theodicy to a temporary halt. In the philosophy of Kant, Fichte and Schelling, at least between 1781 and 1800 – that is, between Kant's *Critique of Pure Reason* and Schelling's *System of Transcendental Idealism* – the problem of theodicy was simply not discussed. It was not discussed because a radical solution had been found for it. The solution was the claim to human autonomy which was proposed in its most extreme form at precisely this time. And that was the point at which the philosophy of history came to birth.[31]

But the philosophy of history was constructed, like its theological antecedent, in the image of a lawsuit. God had been acquitted, but at a price: he was dismissed from the stage. Mankind now claimed the stage as his own. But at a price: Mankind became subject to the accusations previously levelled against God. For if Man is indeed an autonomous and fully responsible being, then he cannot escape the conclusion that he is the author of crimes. He has to face the charge that he has made the historical world in which the experience of evil – the experience of antagonism, antinomy, contradiction – remains.

Having proclaimed himself the author of his own history, Mankind is suddenly afflicted by doubt. His enthusiasm for this newly-won status wanes. He is ill at ease with his new identity; indeed, he begins to have a positive aversion to it. But a stratagem lies ready to hand. He can play a double game. He can distinguish between 'transcendental' man and 'empirical' man.

Hegel and Lukács are the virtuosi of this device; *Die Vernunft in der Geschichte* and *Geschichte und Klassenbewusstsein* their classic performances. If not exactly whisked back into the wings, Mankind is demoted to a sub-plot by Hegel's 'Cunning of Reason'. On this view, those who act in history do indeed achieve their interests, but in doing so they also accomplish something further, something of which they are not aware and which they did not intend. It is of course the World-Spirit which governs the historical process and uses the passions and designs of individuals and nations to bring Its own purposes to fulfilment. Hence Hegel's philosophy of history entails the denial that it is possible to identify, socially and politically, a subject of history. Mankind's identity as the subject of his history is, as it were, suspended. A century later, Lukács produced a variation on the theme. Now it is the Proletariat who is a historical actor with a suspended identity. Lukács knows very well, of course, that there is a difference between the empirical consciousness of the proletariat and what he claims to be its world-historical goal. But he too demotes the empirical subject at the expense of the transcendental subject. What Hegel achieves by inventing the 'Cunning of Reason' Lukács does by resorting to subjunctives. He tells us that the correct consciousness of the proletariat – that is to say, the attainment of its true identity – would be those thoughts 'which men in a particular life-situation *would* have, *if they were able fully to comprehend this situation*'.[32] He bridges the gap between the 'real' and the 'necessary' consciousness of the proletariat, between his empirical and his transcendental subject, with the aid of the party. In the world of allegory, the proletariat, who are hardly yet aware of their historical role and still adhere to bourgeois values, is stylised into the subject of History. In the world of reality, the party undertakes the administration of its class consciousness, so guaranteeing that identity of the subject of History with itself which does not yet empirically exist.

By 1933 this did not sound too convincing. Revolution had been turned into Stalinist bureaucracy in Russia and aborted by Nazi dictatorship in Germany. So the stratagem of distinguishing between the empirical and the transcendental subject of history reappeared in a new variant. It took the form of a division between those, on the one side, who have made history and are able to be held responsible for it, and those, on the other side, who want to make history and who want to be responsible for it. In this conflict between the past and the future, the protagonists of the future feel hindered from achieving their true identity by an obstacle: the obstacle is provided by what at present historically prevails. Naturally, this obstacle provokes their indignation; but it is an indignation buoyed up by a transparent current of enthusiasm. To be the subject of History is to undertake an onerous task. To be hindered from becoming the subject of History is to be relieved of the burden. It is always a help not to be caught napping. Now it is possible to say: we wanted to be the authors of History and we still want to be, but the others were in fact the authors. It is precisely those who call for the liberation of men, those who assert that Mankind achieves its essence, its true identity, in the course of History, who are the most vigilant in searching out these other authors.

So the claim for autonomy ends by reintroducing heteronomy. The accusations against God are replaced by the accusations against the opponent. But to have an opponent is not enough. He must be an enemy whose strength is superior, whose will prevails. Only such an opponent can provide those who proclaim their intention of being the subject of History with the cast-iron alibi which they seek – the security of being able to say that they are not yet the subject of History. The critical theorist seeks discharge from the responsibility which the Enlightenment claim to autonomy has enjoined upon him. So he stalks the opponent whose authority is still unbroken; and – one is tempted to add – the more unbreakable, the better. Only thus can they guarantee their own impotence.

The need for this guarantee is no proof of personal cowardice. It is the unfolding of a necessary logic. In the Frankfurt School the aspirations of the Enlightenment remain but its illusions have been lost. This is not a rejection of the Enlightenment, but an admission of its inner contradiction, the contradiction contained within its claim to autonomy. Critical theory is the Achilles heel of the Enlightenment brought to light.

But the efforts of the Frankfurt School to construct a critical theory of society are undermined from a second direction. The characteristic response of German sociology to the onset of capitalist industrialisation was a mood of tragic pessimism.[33] This found expression in the belief that the new network of institutions produced by men had acquired an autonomy independent of human needs, that they had assumed a dynamism which was hardly any longer susceptible to human control, and that this dynamism worked in direct opposition to the intentions which originally lay behind the creation of these new social structures. This is the characteristic topos of German sociology: the thesis of heteronomy. Means have become ends in themselves. The attitude of tragic pessimism gave rise to a general theory of alienation.

This found succinct expression in Simmel's essay on 'The Concept and Tragedy of Culture'.[34] Simmel there describes what he believes to be an irreconcilable dualism. He views the basic conflict of culture as the completely fundamental antithesis between the principle of life and the principle of form.[35] Life, as process, requires embodiment in objective structures; but these structures, in their stability, are the antithesis of process. So the contents of culture, which are 'originally created by subjects for subjects', through a logic inherent in their nature, 'estrange themselves from their origin as well as from their purpose'[36] in the very process of acquiring objective form. This sets into motion an unending condition of self-estrangement. 'In contrast to life, vibrating, restless, endlessly self-evolving, form ... stands as life's fixed, ideal, and immovable product, whose uncanny counter-effect is to fix, indeed to freeze, all vitality; it is as if the creative motion of the soul were always to die in its products ... This is the real tragedy of culture. For we define a tragic fate ... as one in which the destroying forces are not only directed against a being but originate in the deepest recesses of this very being; it is a fate in which a destiny is completed in a self-destruction which is latent and, so to speak, the logical development of the very structure by means of which that being has attained its positive existence.'[37] From this diagnosis Simmel concludes that the fetishism which Marx had attributed to economic commodities represents only a special case of this general fate of the contents of culture.[38] Marx's analysis is universalised by abstracting it from any specific historical context. In Simmel's view, the opposition within the productive process cannot be resolved, as Marx believed, in a future classless society, because self-division is the universal characteristic of human culture. The motif of impotence which issues from this position had already been formulated, in a more sociologically differentiated manner, six years earlier, in Weber's essay on *The Protestant Ethic*

and the Spirit of Capitalism. Weber's central point was that capitalism, once it had come to rest on a firmly established mechanical
base, severed itself from the psychological preconditions which
were to be found in the beginnings of bourgeois society. The
Puritans wanted to be professional men; we have to be.[39] Part of
Weber's intention was of course to demonstrate that a religious
genealogy formed an essential constituent in the emerging spirit of
capitalism. But it is the change from a world of free professional
men to a world of men for whom professionalism is a new bondage
that constitutes the crux of his whole analysis. Although the
capitalist mode of production had generated the steel-hard shell of
rationality, that shell seemed to Weber to be independent of the
relations of production. Even the elimination of private capitalism
could not now break it down. Such a change, in his opinion, would
mean merely that the state bureaucracy would dominate alone:
somewhat as in Ancient Egypt, except in an incomparably more
rational, and hence inescapable, form.[40] The problem for Weber,
therefore, was 'what we can oppose to this machinery in order to
keep a portion of mankind free from this parcelling-out of the soul,
from the supreme mastery of the bureaucratic way of life'.[41] Unless
charismatic leaders were to emerge, this remnant of humanity
would probably live only in retreat from the public sphere. There
might be, he suggested, 'a retreat of the last and most sublime
values . . . out of the public world . . . into a sphere of mystical life or
into the brotherhood of direct relations of individuals with one
another'.[42]

What was first encountered with tragic pessimism was later
accepted with complacent resignation. In 1961 Schelsky took up
Weber's theme again.[43] He drew attention to the co-operation of
bureaucrats, the military, and politicians which had developed on
a large scale in the period following the Second World War. This
marked a new or second stage of rationality which Schelsky
referred to as the emergence of the 'technical state', the power of
which, he claimed, was now so comprehensive as to bring about
the virtual collapse of all forms of political participation on the part
of citizens. The core of his argument was that political measures
now follow the logic of technical expertise. Since these measures
are proposed by experts and shown to be necessary by those in
possession of technical knowledge, no objection of a strictly political kind could be raised against them. For technical decisions are
self-evident and make political domination, and political education,

superfluous. Political domination, he argued, had been superseded by the administration of things; indeed political opinions and intentions are not so much functionalised as rendered completely functionless. It was in the same year – 1961 – in which Schelsky launched the German technocracy debate,[44] that Gehlen delivered a lecture on 'Cultural Crystallisation'.[45] Its tone differed radically from Weber's impassioned address to the *Verein für Sozialpolitik* in 1909: indeed, these two speeches, separated by half a century, are emblematic of the changed mood within German sociology as a whole. The possibility of any real retreat from the public sphere, or of its transformation by charismatic leaders, had definitely receded. Gehlen announced the end of the epoch of secular ideologies which had begun in 1789. The 'revolutionary systems of ideas since 1789 engaged the individual in a direct capacity for action ... But that corresponded to a more primitive consciousness of the problems of society ... today it has become impossible to draw up a programme which could decisively change the relationships between economic and political life. In the powerful, balanced machine ... such a programme would find no junctures at which it might intervene.'[46] For now a process of cultural crystallisation has taken place. Our culture has reached a point where the basic stock of possibilities inherent in it has been fully articulated; the counter-possibilities and antitheses have been discovered and either accommodated or eliminated. No chance remains of opposing any clearly discernible global alternative to the established system. We have arrived in post-history:[47] history takes place today only as a kind of administered fate. 'At least,' he concedes in a gesture of grandiosely sentimental pathos, 'men are burnt up and consumed by their own creations and not by crude nature, like animals.'[48] But that also means, he claims, that the techniques which men have accumulated should be regarded 'not as the product of human effort for the extension of material power, but rather as a great biological process', since the apparatus, which we once freely operated, now begins to 'belong to our biological life, like the snail's shell to the snail'.[49] For Gehlen the domination of institutions has become so complete that Weber's question – what can we oppose to this machinery in order to keep a remnant of humanity free from the autocracy of bureaucratic rule – is rejected out of hand as a romantic gesture. Weber's stoicism, which was burdened with tragic apprehension, returns in Gehlen with a more resigned yet complacent hue.

Despite their variation in tone and elaboration, these arguments share a common strategic significance. All of them were directed, whether overtly or covertly, against a specific counter-thesis; only from the opposing pressure exerted by this counter-position can their motive force and meaning be understood. German sociology has frequently been interpreted, and may in fact best be viewed, as a series of answers to questions raised by Marx's analysis of the capitalist system of production. This challenge was at once theoretical and practical.[50]

By the end of the nineteenth century Marx's literary executors had made accessible to the public many writings previously forgotten or unobtainable. During Engels' lifetime the manuscripts of the second and third volume of *Capital* and the *Theses on Feuerbach* were published, while *The Poverty of Philosophy* and *Wage Labour and Capital* were republished. Subsequently, Kautsky republished the *Contribution to the Critique of Political Economy* in 1897; Eleanor Marx published *Value, Price and Profit* in 1899; Kautsky's *Neue Zeit*, founded in 1883, made available numerous little-known Marxist texts; and Mehring's four-volume edition of Marx's writings in 1902 included some significant early works like *The Holy Family*, the essay *On the Jewish Question*, and the *Introduction to the Critique of Hegel's Philosophy of Right*. These posthumous publications and republications provided exegetes and critics with a corpus on the basis of which it became for the first time possible to form an estimate of Marx's work as a whole. Commentaries mushroomed correspondingly. According to Sombart's estimate, Marx was hardly read at all in the seventies, and only twenty commentaries on him were available before 1883; but this had increased to 58 between 1884 and 1894, and to no less than 214 between 1895 and 1904.[51]

The practical challenge appeared almost simultaneously, with the emergence in the nineties of the Social Democratic Party as a large, self-contained mass movement, led by Marxist theoreticians like Engels, Liebknecht, Bebel, Bernstein and Kautsky, who had succeeded in securing the adoption of a Marxist ideology in the Erfurt Programme of 1891. True, the progress towards radicalisation ought not to be overestimated: compared with other European countries, Germany enjoyed a substantial degree of internal political stability during the quarter of a century before the outbreak of the First World War.[52] There were no food riots and street fighting, as in Italy in 1898; no nationalist eruptions, such as shook the

Habsburg Empire; no crisis comparable to the Dreyfus Affair in France; nothing comparable to the Russian revolution of 1905; and, in practice, the deterministic interpretation of Marxism elaborated by Kautsky and his followers induced a cautionary strategy bordering on fatalism which, as Korsch was later to remark, amounted to a kind of theoretical defence and metaphysical consolation.[53] Yet the fact remains that no country outside Germany in the nineteenth century possessed a Marxist party so large or so politically significant as the Social Democratic Party; and, although it was unable to break the power of the dominant system, the political subculture of the labour movement was viewed by many as a permanent source of instability within the Reich.

It was in the mid-nineties that German sociologists began to respond to this two-pronged challenge. Until the close of the First World War the chief participants in the discussion were Rudolf Stammler, Georg Simmel, Robert Michels, Ernst Troeltsch, and, above all of course, Werner Sombart and Max Weber; during the twenties the proponents of Wissenssoziologie, such as Karl Mannheim, Max Scheler and Theodor Geiger began to take a prominent part in the debate, as did also conservative intellectuals like Carl Schmitt, Hans Freyer and Ernst Jünger, who were hoping for a revolution from the Right. Many of these discussions were naturally critical, three lines of attack being most commonly employed. It was argued that Historical Materialism was a one-sided, monocausal explanatory schema; that Marx's analysis had conflated the logical distinction between statements of fact and statements of value; and that his specific concept of ideology, while yielding the fruitful general axiom of a correspondence between infrastructure and superstructure, was itself ideological. Yet despite the scope and the sustained force of these attacks, it would be unjust to read the work of the classical German sociologists solely as a set of politically motivated polemics against Historical Materialism.[54] In rendering Marx the tribute of relentless critique they were admitting the extent to which his categories had penetrated their own patterns of thought; when Weber said that 'the intellectual world in which we live is a world moulded to a large degree by Marx and Nietzsche',[55] he was merely stating with characteristic forcefulness what his compatriots tacitly acknowledged.

Above all – and it is here that, as a group, they differed most markedly from their contemporaries in France, Italy, and even Russia[56] – the German sociologists were indebted to Marx in adopting the concept of capitalism as the unifying explanatory principle for the interpretation of their age.[57] When in 1904 Sombart, Weber and Jaffé founded the *Archiv für Sozialwissenschaft und Sozialpolitik*, they announced their intention of treating all aspects of economic and social life from the point of view of the revolutionary process wrought by capitalism.[58] And Naumann drew the appropriate comparison in 1911 when he wrote that 'just as the Frenchman has his theme: what is the great revolution? so we through our national fate have for a long time had as our theme: what is capitalism?'[59] However much they differed among each other over the practical political consequences which they inferred from their specific sociological analyses, the generation of sociologists of which Weber was the outstanding representative were at one in focusing their attention on the problem of capitalism. All of them had assimilated the set of concepts with which Marx had defined the essential features of the capitalist system: the private ownership of the means of production and the origin of profit from this property system; the propelling force of science and technology; and the class struggle. And all of them sought to elaborate the differences between, and the specific characteristics of, different historical epochs in terms of the development of different types of economic organisation.

But in assimilating Marx's bequest they transformed it in such a way as to conflate the features specific to the capitalist system of production with the features of instrumental rationality. This process of conflation was reinforced by a characteristic procedure of argument by analogy. Tönnies' classic distinction between 'Gemeinschaft' and 'Gesellschaft' set the tone. The nuclear forms of Gemeinschaft, which refers to 'an original and essential unity between men',[60] are found in 'motherly, sexual, and brotherly and sisterly love';[61] the paradigm of Gesellschaft is 'the act of exchange, where it appears in its purest form insofar as it is performed by individuals who are strangers to each other and have nothing in common, and thus essentially are antagonistic or even opposed to one another'.[62] The trajectory of all previous history marks the route from Gemeinschaft to Gesellschaft, the 'irresistible tendency towards the rationalization of all relations'.[63] This historical trend appears economically, in the displacement of the natural economy by the money economy; legally, in the transformation of familial into contractual relations; politically, in the unification of all political power, all relationships of authority based on prescriptive

right into the legislative power of the centralised state; and conceptually, in the opposition and struggle of religious and scientific
consciousness,[64] for 'scientific concepts assume the same position
in a scientific system as commodities do in the Gesellschaft'.[65]
Simmel's homologies between the historical development of law,
intellectuality, and money entail a similar analytical strategy. All
three are characterised by 'indifference to individual qualities', by
extracting from the concrete fullness of life some 'abstract,
general factor';[66] and in this they are representative of the intellectual operations with the aid of which the modern age regulates the
world: the process of calculating rationality. 'Its epistemological
ideal is to conceive of the world as a great arithmetical sum, to
collect the processes and qualitative characteristics of things into a
system of numbers.'[67] Simmel notes the connection between calculating rationality and the money economy; indeed, he asserts
that 'it was the money economy which first brought into practical
life ... the ideal of numerical calculability',[68] and that it necessarily
conduces to the spread of mathematical operations and the reduction of all qualitative to quantitative values. But the effect of his
analogical procedure is to leave the specific nature of the causal
relationship between the money economy and instrumental
rationality unclear. On this crucial question his embarrassment is
quite explicit. Rationality, he suggests, 'seems to me to stand in
close causal connection with the money economy'.[69] Yet to this
close causal connection he devotes one paragraph in a 500 page
study on *Die Philosophie des Geldes*. Weber's taxonomic method
likewise accentuates homologies between distinguishable aspects
of social reality, if at a more systematic and differentiated level. He
freely acknowledges the separation of the worker from the means of
production, but he subsumes the characteristics of capitalism
within the dominant perspective of rationality, stressing the
similarities between the modern state and the capitalist enterprise:
the whole developmental history of the modern state in particular
is identical with the history of modern officialdom and bureaucratic enterprise, just as the whole development of high capitalism
is identical with increasing bureaucratisation of the economic
enterprise.[70] This analysis found an appropriate pendant in
Schelsky's essay of 1961 on *Der Mensch in der wissenschaftlichen
Zivilisation*.[71] The defining feature of contemporary society is here
seen as a universal technology in which three spheres of application may be distinguished.[72] First, there are the techniques of

production, the creation of material goods; secondly, there are the techniques of organisation, the methods of social control; and thirdly, there is human technology, that is the techniques for controlling, changing and inducing specific effects in the emotional and intellectual life of man. This tripartite distinction, in which parity of significance is assigned to each of the three components, is the natural issue of the characteristically German sociological response to industrialisation. At the outset, the essence of capitalism is ostensibly grasped, but without entering into its specific economic problems, above all the problem of surplus value; the procedure of analogy tendentially usurps the work of establishing causal connections; and eventually, given the initial conflation of capitalist production and instrumental rationality, the balance of emphasis comes to be tilted inexorably towards the second of the two terms in the analysis.

The effects of this intellectual subsidence resonate throughout the work of critical theory; they appear variously in Adorno, in Marcuse, and in Habermas.

It is true that Adorno sometimes states or implies that capitalism, and not instrumental rationality, is the enemy, as for instance when he asserts that although 'interested parties explain the culture industry in technological terms', they make no mention of the fact 'that the basis on which technology acquires power over society is the power of those whose economic hold over society is greatest',[73] so that the preferred technological rationale is 'the result not of a law of movement in technology as such but of its function in today's economy'.[74] Again, at the Congress in Frankfurt in 1968, he opted for 'late capitalism' rather than 'industrial society' as the appropriate characterisation of the contemporary world, on the ground that the concept of industrial society merely alluded to the possibility of a rational application of productive forces, whereas the concept of late capitalism expressed the reality of the system: that is, the reality of the relations of production which perpetuate internalised coercion instead of fostering real emancipation.[75] Yet such arguments are residues of an allegiance which was fundamentally undermined by the analysis contained both in the *Dialectic of Enlightenment* and in *Negative Dialectics*. For whereas Marx had connected the principle of commodity exchange with a specific system of property ownership, Adorno detaches commodity exchange from a particular historical type of economic organisation, and views it instead as the most complete expression of instrumental rationality. The essential distinction between Marx and Adorno is that the latter traces domination back to the use of concepts. The concept as such is viewed as an instrumental accomplishment by means of which men define the world in accordance with their will to control it. To this end everything is submitted to the rule of identity; that is, the rule according to which classes of objects are constructed and all particulars are subsumed under such classes as examples; hence the particular can make its appearance only as something which is already predefined by the concept to which it has been assigned.[76] Adorno concludes by suggesting an affinity between this form of instrumental rationality and the structure of the capitalist economy in terms which unmistakably echo those of Tönnies and Simmel: 'Bourgeois society is dominated by the law of equivalence. What is heterogeneous is made comparable by being reduced to abstract magnitudes.'[77]

Marcuse, likewise, adheres in part to the traditional Marxist analysis. He affirms that the antagonism between productive forces and productive relations continues to exist within the capitalist system, for which the profit mechanism remains the guiding principle: 'Even in the most highly organised form of capitalism the social need for private appropriation and distribution of profit remains the regulator of the economy.'[78] And he stresses that the planned obsolescence of material resources and productivity is a necessary, and not an accidental, feature of the system: late industrial society has increased rather than diminished the need for parasitic and alienated functions.[79] But once more these propositions are undercut by the basic thrust of his analysis, which deflects attention from the relations of production and focuses instead on the technologically most advanced methods of production. The adoption of technological rationality as the key concept suggests that the generation of mass welfare and the manufacture of total annihilation are co-ordinated into a profitable system whose dynamic knows no inherent limits. This issues in an analysis which bears remarkable affinities with those propounded by sociologists of the Right like Schelsky: according to both diagnoses, the structure of authority in advanced industrial society is no longer described in terms of a theory of classes or elites but in the categories of technology and administrative rationality.[80] But given Marcuse's continuing allegiance to substantial elements of Marx's analysis, his own thesis of technological rationality becomes internally incoherent. For if it is to be taken literally, it implies an identity between the logic of the capitalist productive process and the logic of technological development; whereas the very facts of waste production and planned obsolescence to which he points clearly demonstrate that no such identity in fact exists. In effect Marcuse is not so much concerned to show how technology acts as an instrument of political or economic power, but rather to suggest, like Adorno, that it is intrinsically an instrument of domination. This emerges at times in *One-Dimensional Man*,[81] but appeared more clearly in his famous attack on Weber at the Heidelberg Congress of 1964, when he suggested that 'the very concept of technical reason is perhaps ideological. Not only the application of technology but technology is domination ... methodical, scientific, calculated, calculating control. Specific purposes and interests of domination are not foisted upon technology "subsequently" and from the outside; they enter the very construction of the technical apparatus ... Such a "purpose" of domination is "substantive" and to this extent belongs to the very form of technical reason.'[82]

While criticising the imprecision of Marcuse's suggestion, Habermas has sought to develop it more systematically in his concept of instrumental action. It is true, once again, that this new position is modulated by a continuing adherence to parts of Marx's heritage. In the sixties, Habermas attacked the technocratic determinists on the ground that they assumed an immanent necessity of technical progress, which owes its appearance of being an independent, self-regulating process only to the way in which social interests operate in it;[83] while more recently he has suggested that late capitalist systems are threatened by a breakdown in legitimation, manifest particularly in crises of motivation: that is, in discrepancies between the need for motives which the state and the occupational system announce, on the one hand, and the offer of motivation on the part of the socio-cultural system, on the other.[84] But he has arrived at this point only after having explicitly discarded two essential constituents of Marx's analysis. He denied, first, that an analysis of contemporary society could be constructed as a critique of political economy; the separation of the state from society characteristic of liberal capitalism having been superseded by a reciprocal interlocking of the two, state and society no longer stand in the relationship of superstructure to base; but a method of analysis which methodically isolates at the outset the laws of motion of the economy can only claim to comprehend this society in its essential structures as long as politics are dependent on the economic base.[85] And he then denied that Marx's theory of class struggle was applicable to state-regulated capitalism; for the system of advanced capitalism is so defined by a policy of securing the loyalty of the wage-earning masses through rewards, that is, by avoiding conflict, that the conflict still built into the structure of society by virtue of the private mode of capital utilisation is the very area of conflict which has the greatest possibility of remaining latent.[86] His main focus has been directed, instead, to the conflict between communicative and instrumental action; he wants to draw attention to the human interests which are served by natural and human science, and to their respective criteria of success and failure. He claims that in natural science the 'interest' is in technical control so that the character of natural science as value-free is viewed as a value characteristic derived from the human decision to develop a form of knowledge which is technically exploitable.[87] This does not mean that the community of scientists are consciously or directly interested in technical control; for although whole branches of theoretical science are in fact supported by industry today, this historical development made its appearance no more than a century ago. Nor is his main aim to argue, like Chomsky, that scientific research establishments, universities and technical institutions form a military–industrial complex which can be deployed by political elites for pursuing global ends. What Habermas calls interest cannot be experienced as such; it is an interest in which no one may be interested in any empirically demonstrable way. His claim that natural science is guided by 'interest in possible technical control' can only be understood in the sense that this interest is the condition of the possibility of natural science. That is to say, he is claiming that it is not merely the emergence and continued existence of science, but also its procedure and methodological structure, which must be explained by such an interest. So that if this claim is to be made good, it must be demonstrated that there is a systematic relationship between, on the one hand, the logical structure of natural science, and, on the other hand, the pragmatic structure of the possible applications of the information generated within this framework.[88]

In Habermas, as in Marcuse and Adorno, the problem of allegiance to a unified and coherent frame of reference recurs, each time in a new variant. The exponential development and diffusion of science and technology bring all of them to a radical revision of the critique of capitalism which had been adopted by critical theory at the point of its inception. Since science and technology are no longer simply elements within the work process but have become the primary productive force, a self-reinforcing circle has been set in motion: society is made increasingly dependent on applied science, and then scientific criteria are appealed to in order to decide whether or not the social world is rationally organised. Hence the growing awareness in the Western world as a whole that it is becoming increasingly necessary to distinguish between the truly liberating effects of natural science, and the use of scientific empiricism, together with the language of pseudo-science, to underwrite particular distributions of social power. To this new awareness critical theory has made a notable contribution by drawing attention to the way in which modern science and technology have generated mechanisms for justifying the organisation of society. But they have been unable to demonstrate the precise connection between the development of technology and the structure of the capitalist economy. Hence their view of the capitalist productive system becomes as equivocal as their standpoint *vis-à-vis* the Enlightenment philosophy of history.

As they have chosen to deploy it, therefore, their initial paradigm, Marx's *Critique of Political Economy*, becomes vulnerable on its two flanks. The concept of critique is compromised by its ties with the myth of Enlightenment, the view of history as one all-embracing process in which a historical subject attains its essence, autonomy. And the critique of political economy is compromised by a vision of heteronomy peculiar to German social theory, issuing from its characteristic conflation of features specific to the capitalist process of production and features specific to instrumental rationality. It is by the combined pressure of this intellectual pincer-movement that the work of critical theory, viewed as a general strategy for the construction of a theory of contemporary society, is permanently exposed to the threat of conceptual erosion

8

Conclusion

Such unity as may exist among the chief exponents of critical theory cannot be found at the level of explicit political belief and prescription. It is true that the period following the Second World War saw a marked convergence in the views of Horkheimer and Adorno when they came increasingly to look to the individual sphere as the only viable point of resistance to the 'administered world'. This position was expressed in the Preface to Adorno's *Minima Moralia*, where he stated that 'in view of the totalitarian unanimity which cries out for the eradication of difference directly as meaning, some of the liberating social forces may even temporarily come together in the sphere of the individual';[1] and the thought was echoed a decade later when Horkheimer admitted that 'our hope rests in the work to ensure that in the beginning of a world period dominated by blocks of administered men, a few will be found who will offer up some resistance'.[2] Not surprisingly, he hesitated before agreeing to the republication of the early essays; dominated as they were by economic and political ideas which no longer had any direct application, the essays of the thirties could be offered in 1968 only as 'documentation'.[3] When, in the same year, Marcuse reissued his pre-war essays, he was just as emphatic in drawing attention to the unbridgeable abyss which separated the thirties and the sixties.[4] But, unlike both Horkheimer and Adorno, he was still engaged during the sixties in exploring new possibilities of radical practice; the rise of a number of non-Marxist, non-proletarian, and sometimes even non-political movements, especially in the United States – the Campaign for Black Civil Rights, the Anti-Vietnam War Campaign, the 'drop-out' phenomenon, the Women's Liberation Movement – seemed to him to provide new impulses and forms of radical practice. In his inaugural lecture at Frankfurt in 1965, Habermas made a point of connecting up the schematic statement of his own position with the project sketched out by Horkheimer in his programmatic statement of 1937.[5] Yet he also analysed elsewhere the collapse of the liberal concept of publicity in a work whose political emphases are at odds with the preoccupation of the older representatives of critical theory in at least one significant respect. What is entirely lacking in his otherwise exemplary study, *Strukturwandel der Öffentlichkeit*, is any consideration of that phase in the development of capitalist society in which the bourgeois public world collapsed in face of fascist terror. In a work conceived within the tradition of critical theory this is a remarkable lacuna: for Horkheimer, Adorno and Marcuse the discussion of fascism had been the driving motive behind their analysis of the mass media.

If no unity can be found among the main proponents of critical theory in the form of an explicit system of political argument or belief, it must be located at some other level. For to consider the work of these four writers in relation to each other is to presume, implicitly if not explicitly, that a unified point of reference does exist, that there is in fact a specific object of study common to all of them. To produce an expository and comparative study of some of their works is no epistemologically innocent enterprise. It necessarily raises the question of the possibility of the apparently routine and taken-for-granted activities of exposition and comparison. If, as here, several texts and thinkers are involved, the question must arise: what is the basis of the comparability of these texts and thinkers? The fact that they happen to be generally acknowledged as in need of the same covering epithet – critical theory – merely begs the question. Comparability is no more given in the nature of reality than marriage vows flow from a certain convergence of interest. Comparability demands, here, that we know the system of concepts and the object thought by them, in the case of each of the thinkers concerned. That is to say, we must know the problematic. To compare thinkers is to ask, implicitly if not explicitly, whether the object of these thinkers' works are the same or different objects.

It has already been suggested that anyone who seeks to answer this question will encounter some embarrassments. It can be said, in a very general sense, that each of the thinkers here considered – Horkheimer, Adorno, Marcuse and Habermas – have produced a critique of domination. But we run into difficulties as soon as we try to answer the question: domination by what? For the attempt to construct a coherent critical model constantly breaks down, and this for two reasons of a general nature, each of which reinforces the other. The concept of critique is compromised by its links with a view of history which envisages a single, all-embracing process in which a historical subject attains its essence, autonomy. And the concept of domination is compromised by the conflation, peculiar to German social theory, of features specific to the capitalist process of production and features specific to instrumental rationality. These two currents interlock. It was the task of the German philosophy of history to elaborate the claim to human autonomy: to demonstrate that it is Man Himself who makes his world, that all which appears to be imposed upon him from outside must be recognised as his own deed. But this claim to autonomy bears the irremovable traces of the heritage which it seeks to disown; this is a theological heritage, and it foundered, in the last third of the eighteenth century, on the problem of evil. Thus the claim for autonomy ended by *reintroducing heteronomy*. But the thesis of heteronomy was the leitmotif of German sociology. On this view, means have become ends in themselves: a network of institutions produced by men has acquired an autonomy independent of their producers, a dynamism which is hardly any longer susceptible to human control and which frequently works in direct opposition to the intention present at their conception. The generalised theory of alienation in which this position issues *reinforces* the collapse of the claim to autonomy. Through this combined pressure, critical theory is exposed to the threat of erosion by its assimilated metaphysical and sociological ballast.

It is, nonetheless, possible to extricate a body of specific propositions from this enveloping orgy of abstractions, to find the basis for the comparability of the texts in question, and in this way to pinpoint more precisely their strengths and weaknesses.

The basis of comparability resides in the fact that all four writers considered here have produced critiques, in the sense that they have studied the methods by means of which systems of social constraints become *internalised*. Initially they demonstrated that the transmission of electronic messages extended the power of ideologies beyond the reach of discursive propositions. Both political propaganda and marketing psychology reach down into areas of individual life to exploit personal conflicts or to awaken artificial needs in support of a particular social system. By blurring the distinction between the private and the institutionalised, they make it more difficult to separate internal desire and external suggestion. It was this which highlighted the new capacity of ideologies to dispense with systems of explanatory concepts: to internalise public constraints by reducing the explicit ideological distance between concepts and the circumstances to which concepts referred. Subsequently, in *Dialectic of Enlightenment*, Horkheimer and Adorno argued that the exploitation of external nature for the purpose of freeing men from subjection to it strikes back in the repression of man's instinctual nature. Nature – his own as well as that of the external world – is 'given' to the ego as something that has to be conquered. Intellectualised passion drives out sensuousness, and leads to its expression in distorted forms. Man's control over himself, which grounds his selfhood, therefore entails the mutilation of the subject in whose service it is undertaken. Ritual sacrifices are superseded by instinctual sacrifices. Through the internalisation of rationalised social constraints, sacrifice is introjected as renunciation. Later, Marcuse went on to show how social constraints could be introjected in a society which ostensibly loosens the burdens of instinctual renunciation. Under affluent capitalism, those who are constitutionally free are libidinally bound to the commodity-form. Below the level of conscious ideology, the human organism is trained to recieve certain stimuli and to repel others; patterns of organic reaction are implanted in individuals, so setting in motion a dynamic that internally inhibits possible liberation. Finally, Habermas sees a process of internalised constraint at work in the form of a new, technocratic ideology. Unlike the old ideologies this is not an illusion, a projection of the good life; it is not a collective wish-fulfilment, nor a rationalisation in the Freudian sense of that term. It does not embody a split between a moral sphere and some other sphere. It aims at the repression of the explicitly moral sphere as such. Since science and technology are no longer simply elements within the work process but have become the primary productive force, a self-reinforcing circle is set in motion: society is made more and more dependent on applied science, and then scientific criteria are appealed to in order to decide whether or not the social world is rationally organised.

If the strength of these arguments derives from their demonstration of the ways in which social constraints are internalised, their weakness resides in an appeal to a critical public *which is never firmly localised*. Initially, Horkheimer envisaged a form of theory in which practice was a constitutive element. Critical theory sought to eliminate an opposition within the theorist himself. The scholarly specialist 'as a scientist' regards social reality as extrinsic to him, and 'as a citizen' he exercises his interest in it through political articles, membership in political parties, and participation in elections; but he does not unify these two activities except, at best, by psychological interpretation. Critical theory aims to go beyond this opposition within each theoretician between the 'scientist' and the 'citizen'; it has a concept of man as being in conflict with himself until that opposition has been removed. But this theoretical postulate was never publicly anchored. Horkheimer's position was first crystallised not in the form of the explicit assumption of a politically revolutionary standpoint, but rather as the negative expression of revulsion against capitalist repression. It proposed no means of establishing specific, organisational links with the working class of its native country; and it was never articulated in terms of any particular political organisation. Subsequently, Adorno and Horkheimer saw that technological society, by treating nature as transformable matter, created a man-made environment from which the explicit ascription of meanings tended to be eliminated; and they saw that it generated an industrially produced publicity in which forms of synthetic mutuality were fabricated through the electronic transmission of messages. But they failed to underline the equally important fact that technological society necessarily entails a process of privatisation, the erosion of public meanings and the retreat into a world of private meanings. This process of privatisation makes it more difficult to perceive that all social formations, including those characteristic of technologically advanced societies, must still, in principle, presuppose intersubjective rules. Yet their own analysis reproduces the blocking out of public meanings. Their construction of a philosophy of history articulated around the two abstracted concepts of the self and nature itself involves a reductive treatment of intersubjectivity. Later, Marcuse recognised that in political systems generally regarded as democratic, capitalist societies provided certain conditions indispensable for the formation of a critical public by incorporating the principle of toleration into the political constitution. Yet their affluence makes it possible to harness instinctual drives to the goals of the productive system and so undercuts the possible formation of this critical public. But, by envisaging the primary conflict as taking place between technological rationality and latent human needs, Marcuse himself once more curtails the dimension of intersubjectivity. His appeal to biological needs remains abstract so long as it is impossible to specify those areas or institutions within the structure of advanced technological societies in which these needs exert a penetrative and transformative effect as social interests. Finally, Habermas attempts to open out critical theory once more to a public dimension by demonstrating that even the exact methods of natural science must presuppose the interpretation of meanings, an exchange between men in a community of interpretation. The construction of formalised scientific languages is an indirect way of improving natural language communication, and always presupposes intersubjective communication. Yet his position is vulnerable at the point where he borrows a psychoanalytic model in order to argue that a process of self-education in society is conceivable in analogy to the process of self-reflection in individuals. This transfer of the psychoanalytic model to larger groups is problematic. In individual therapy, the aim of the doctor is to help the patient to free himself from internalised constraints. Whereas what obtains in a situation of social conflict is quite the reverse: here there is a condition of reciprocal resistance. The common purpose, which may be assumed within the psycho-analytic situation, is absent in social conflict. The appeal of critical theory to a dimension of public criticism is once again lamed by a form of abstract subjectivism.

The appeal to a critical public sphere which is never securely localised bears the unmistakable traces of a particular national history. The specifically German approach to the problems of the public world is intelligible only in the light of the belated, and constantly disturbed, consolidation of their nation-state. Her western neighbours, who had industrialised earlier and who had already experienced a revolutionary prehistory, had achieved a measure of political stability before the divisive force of capitalist industrialisation threatened their society with the antagonism of capital and labour. But in Germany the development towards the condition of a nation-state took place during a period of accelerated industrialisation. Its uprooting force encountered a world still living within the social framework of traditions which bore the stamp of feudal authority, a world which had not undergone the experience of political revolution. After the political capitulation of the bourgeoisie in the 1848 Revolution and the ensuing integration of substantial elements of the bourgeoisie into the military–feudal power elite, no political force existed in Germany throughout the second half of the nineteenth century which might have been strong enough to carry through a liberal-parliamentary revolution. The currents of power flowed in the opposite direction. As the class opposition between bourgeoisie and proletariat became ever more accentuated, the bourgeoisie were increasingly inclined to arrest parliamentary-democratic developments at the stage reached in 1848. The relatively well-functioning state bureaucracy was ready to foster capitalist development and so made it easier for the bourgeoisie to become reconciled with the traditional, quasi-absolutist political system. During the last third of the nineteenth century German capitalism was at a stage where parliament exercised no decisive function in adjusting competing capitalist interests with each other and with the state bureaucracy. In a state where the economy was becoming monopolised and class conflict politicised, parliament exerted no significant political power.[6] Thus the belated approximation of German conditions to those operative in her western neighbours remained an approximation largely restricted to the technical and legal spheres of the administrations; what was lacking was the enlightenment heritage of political humanism – as distinct from philosophical idealism – and the experience of bourgeois revolution. This distinctive national trajectory was reinforced by the aftermath of the First World War. Because of the shortage of economic resources, and especially raw materials, the First World War rapidly led in Germany to the reshaping of an economic system, previously organised as a market economy, towards a more centrally administered economy. The already manifest presence of the state in economic affairs developed into a comprehensive, military–bureaucratic regime which tended to co-ordinate the whole productive apparatus; the boundary line between the spheres of the state and private economy were ever more effaced.[7] This process of exponential politicisation, the amplification of the public world as a fact, culminated in fascism. The trauma left behind a deep ambivalence among the critical intelligentsia in Germany when faced with the problem of political opposition. In contrast to the stance of French political intellectuals, there was lacking in Germany an unbroken tradition of resistance, and hence the preconditions for a critical discussion of the historical legitimacy of public force. The experience of fascism reinforced this absence; it appears to have suggested that collective political practice is necessarily destructive of critical awareness. Hence the fear that socialist action from the left might set loose precisely that which they oppose – the potential of fascist terror from the right. One of the negative legacies of German fascism was the inclination to regard any form of overt political practice as a form of blind activity.

The western concept of publicity, where publicity is viewed as embodying a value, as referring to the claims and strategies of political activity exercised by responsible citizens, achieved only limited acceptance in Germany. There, the characteristic approach to the problems of the public world have remained encumbered by a vision which sees in public life a diversion from everything which is essentially human, a zone of activity in which men necessarily become estranged from themselves. The public sphere appears problematic because, with the development towards an advanced capitalist society, the amplification of the public world as a fact is in disjunction to the limited sense of the public world as incorporating a value. Fascism was the embodiment of this disjunction in its most brutal form. Here the contradiction was embodied by a process of grotesque inversion: the public world came to be viewed as a sphere in which human finitude was transcended in a quasi-religious fulfilment, the mirage of wholeness in which the disjunction between fact and value was ostensibly eliminated while being effectively demonstrated. Critical theory was the theoretical response to this historical conjuncture. From this derive both its strength and its weakness – its analysis of the methods by which social constraints are internalised, and its appeal to a critical public which is never securely located. The experience of fascism therefore yielded an ambivalent legacy. It afforded a critical insight into the hermetically sealed, coercive force of highly industrialised class societies and the decline of bourgeois individuality; but because of the conditions produced by fascism the possibilities of organising the working class could not enter as a constitutive element into the theory. Critical theory draws its power and its deficiency from this particular incongruity: the incongruity between publicity as a penetrative fact, and publicity as a tenuous value.

NOTES

Chapter One

1 T. W. Adorno et al., *Der Positivismusstreit in der deutschen Soziologie* (Neuwied/Berlin 1969).

2 *Die Linke antwortet Habermas* (Frankfurt 1969).

3 J. Habermas, 'Nachgeahmte Substantialität', in *Philosophisch-politische Profile* (Frankfurt 1971), 200–21; A. Gehlen, *Moral und Hypermoral* (Frankfurt 1969); for a critical overview see W. Lepenies, 'Anthropology and Social Criticism: A view on the Controversy between Arnold Gehlen and Jürgen Habermas', *The Human Context*, **3** (1971), 205–25.

4 J. Habermas, 'Zu Gadamers "Wahrheit und Methode"', and "Der Universalitätsanspruch der Hermeneutik"', in *Hermeneutik und Ideologiekritik* (Frankfurt 1971), 45–56; 120–59.

5 J. Habermas, N. Luhmann, *Theorie der Gesellschaft oder Sozialtechnologie – Was leistet die Systemforschung?* (Frankfurt 1971).

6 See O. Negt, *Politik als Protest* (Frankfurt 1971); A. Kluge, O. Negt, *Öffentlichkeit und Erfahrung, Zur Organisationsanalyse von bürgerlicher und proletarischer Öffentlichkeit* (Frankfurt 1973); H. Holzer, *Gescheiterte Aufklärung? Politik, Ökonomie und Kommunikation in der Bundesrepublik Deutschlands* (München 1971); F. Dröge, *Wissen ohne Bewusstsein – Materialien zur Medienanalyse* (Frankfurt 1972).

7 H. Lubacsz, Review of M. Jay, 'The Dialectical Imagination', *History and Theory* (1975) 202 ff.

8 See F. L. Neumann, 'The Social Sciences', in W. R. Crawford (ed.), *The Cultural Migration. The European Scholar in America* (Philadelphia 1953), 4–26.

9 Ibid.

10 E. Bloch, 'Ungleichzeitigkeit und Pflicht zu ihrer Dialektik' in *Erbschaft dieser Zeit* (Frankfurt 1962), 104–64.

11 See W. J. Mommsen, *Die Geschichtswissenschaft jenseits des Historismus* (Düsseldorf 1972), 24 ff.

12 T. W. Adorno et al., *Der Positivismusstreit in der deutschen Soziologie* (Neuwied/Berlin 1969).

13 See *Die Linke antwortet Habermas* (Frankfurt 1969).

14 See A. & M. Mitscherlich, *Die Unfähigkeit zu trauern* (München 1967).

15 T. W. Adorno (with E. Frenkel-Brunswick, D. T. Levinson, R. Newitt Sandford), *The Authoritarian Personality* (New York 1950).

16 T. W. Adorno, *Philosophie der neuen Musik* (Frankfurt 1958).

17 T. Mann, *The Genesis of a Novel*, tr. by R. and C. Winton (London 1961), 176.

18 T. W. Adorno, *Noten zur Literatur*, 3 Bde. (Frankfurt 1958–64).

19 T. W. Adorno, *Minima Moralia* (Frankfurt 1951).

20 T. Mann, *The Genesis of a Novel* (London 1961), 39–40.

21 T. W. Adorno, *The Jargon of Authenticity*, tr. K. Tarnowski and F. Will (London 1973).

22 M. Horkheimer, 'Traditionelle und Kritische Theorie', in *Kritische Theorie*, **2**, Hg. A. Schmidt, (Frankfurt 1968), 137–91.

23 See G. Röttgers, *Kritik und Praxis* (Berlin 1975), 19.

24 Ibid., 19–20.

25 R. Kosellek, *Kritik und Krise*, (Freiberg/München 1959), 88 ff.

26 P. Bayle, *Dictionnaire Historique et Critique* (3e ed. Rotterdam 1720), 1900.

27 Ibid.

28 R. Kosellek, *Kritik und Krise*, 92.

29 Ibid, 94.

30 J. Habermas, *Strukturwandel der Öffentlichkeit* (Neuwied/Berlin 1969), 11–116.

31 See R. Kosellek, Ibid. 96.

32 Ibid. 126.

33 Ibid. 85.

34 Ibid. 208–9, 213–14; see also 124–7, 132–3, 143–6.

35 See G. Röttgers, *Kritik und Praxis* (Berlin 1975), 45–6.

36 See G. Röttgers, *Kritik und Praxis* (Berlin 1975), 147–9.

37 See H. Marcuse, *Reason and Revolution* (London 1968), 114 ff.

38 See J. Habermas, 'A Postscript to "Knowledge and Human Interests"', *Philosophy of the Social Sciences*, **3** (1973), 157–89.

Chapter Two

1 Now collected together in M. Horkheimer, *Kritische Theorie*, 2 Bds. Hg. A. Schmidt (Frankfurt 1968).

2 M. Horkheimer, 'Bemerkungen über Wissenschaft und Krise', in *Kritische Theorie*, **I**, 1–8.

3 *KT*, **I**, 6.

4 *KT*, **I**, 2.

5 *KT*, **I**, 6.

6 *KT*, **I**, 7.

7 *KT*, **I**, 4.

8 *KT*, **I**, 7.

9 *KT*, **I**, 6.

10 *KT*, **I**, 138 ff, *KT*, **I**, 263 ff.

11 *KT*, **I**, 173 ff.

12 See H. Dubiel, 'Dialektische Wissenschaftskritik und interdisziplinäre Sozialforschung. Theorie und Organisationsstruktur des Frankfurter Instituts für Sozialforschung', *Kölner Zeitschrift für Soziologie und Sozialpsychologie* (1974), 237–66.

13 *KT*, **II**, 192.

14 *KT*, **II**, 158.

15 K. Marx, *Capital* (Moscow 1965), **I**, 183–4.

16 *KT*, **II**, 155.
17 *KT*, **II**, 155.
18 *KT*, **II**, 156–7.
19 *KT*, **II**, 146.
20 *KT*, **II**, 159.
21 *KT*, **II**, 146.
22 *KT*, **II**, 158.
23 *KT*, **II**, 164.
24 *KT*, **II**, 162.
25 *KT*, **II**, 163.
26 *KT*, **II**, 163.
27 *KT*, **II**, 164.
28 *KT*, **II**, 164.
29 *KT*, **II**, 165.
30 *KT*, **II**, 192.
31 *KT*, **II**, 174–5.
32 *KT*, **II**, 174–5.
33 *KT*, **II**, 155.
34 M. Horkheimer, 'Die gegenwärtige Lage der Sozialphilosophie und die Aufgaben eines Instituts für Sozialforschung' in Ibid. *Sozialphilosophische Studien* (Frankfurt 1972), 34.
35 Ibid. 32.
36 M. Horkheimer, *Zeitschrift für Sozialforschung*, 1 (1932), 111.
37 See Perry Anderson, *Considerations on Western Marxism* (London 1976).
38 *KT*, **II**, 195.
39 *KT*, **II**, 182.
40 *KT*, **II**, 182.
41 *KT*, **II**, 186.
42 *KT*, **II**, 186.
43 *KT*, **II**, 186.
44 *KT*, **II**, 187.
45 *KT*, **II**, 182.
46 *KT*, **II**, 182.
47 *KT*, **II**, 186.

Chapter Three

1 See his letter of 22 Feb. 1858, in Marx/Engels, *Werke*, **19** (Berlin 1969), 131–42.
2 See J. Habermas, *Strukturwandel der Öffentlichkeit* (Neuwied/Berlin 1969).
3 K. Marx, *Das Kapital* (Berlin 1957), **1**, 90–1.
4 See J. Matzner, 'Der Begriff der Charaktermaske bei Marx', *Soziale Welt*, **15** (1964).
5 G. Lukács, *Geschichte und Klassenbewusstsein* (Neuwied/Berlin 1967), 442.
6 Ibid. 486.
7 Ibid. 444.
8 Ibid. 440–1.
9 G. Lukács, *Taktik und Ethik*, reprinted in *Wissenschaftlicher Intelligenz, Schulung, Organizationsfrage* (Rotes Presse-Syndikat), 33 ff.

10 G. Lukács, *Geschichte und Klassenbewusstsein*, 224.

11 Ibid. 248.

12 Ibid. 223.

13 Ibid. 219.

14 M. Horkheimer, *Kritische Theorie*, **I**, 286.

15 *KT*, **I**, 286.

16 *KT*, **I**, 337.

17 *KT*, **I**, 337.

18 *KT*, **I**, 340.

19 *KT*, **I**, 340–1.

20 *KT*, **I**, 338.

21 T. W. Adorno, 'Sociology and Psychology', *New Left Review*, **46** (1967).

22 T. W. Adorno, 'Postskriptum', in *Aufsätze zur Gesellschaftstheorie* (Frankfurt 1970), 55.

23 T. W. Adorno, *Stichworte* (Frankfurt 1969), 183.

24 T. W. Adorno, *Negative Dialektik* (Frankfurt 1966), 343.

25 See J. Orr, 'German Social Theory and the Hidden Face of Technology', *Archives européennes de sociologie*, **XV** (1974), 312–36.

26 M. Horkheimer and T. W. Adorno, 'Ideology', in *Aspects of Sociology*, tr. J. Viertel (London 1973), 189.

27 Ibid. 190.

28 T. W. Adorno, *Gesammelte Schriften*, Hg. R. Tiedemann, **9** (Frankfurt 1975), 401.

29 Ibid. 398, 416.

30 Ibid. 399.

31 Ibid. 404, 409.

32 Ibid. 404, 409.

33 C. S. Steinberg, *The Mass Communicators* (New York 1958), 122.

34 See J. Habermas, *Strukturwandel der Öffentlichkeit* (Neuwied/Berlin 1961), passim.

35 L. W. Doob, *Public Opinion and Propaganda* (New York 1948), 35.

36 W. Albig, *Public Opinion* (New York 1938).

37 M. B. Ogle, *Public Opinion and Political Dynamics* (Boston 1958), 48.

38 L. W. Doob, *Public Opinion and Propaganda* (New York 1948), 35: 'In this sense it might appear as though public opinion exists whenever people have attitudes.'

39 E. L. Bernays, ed. *The Engineering of Consent* (Oklahoma 1955).

Chapter Four

1 M. Horkheimer, T. W. Adorno, *Dialektik der Aufklärung* (Frankfurt 1969), 1; *Dialectic of Enlightenment*, tr. J. Cumming (London 1973), xi.

2 M. Horkheimer, *Kritische Theorie*, **I** (Frankfurt 1968), 1.

3 M. Horkheimer, *Kritische Theorie*, **11** (Frankfurt 1968), 193; 306.

4 *DA*, 27–8; *DE*, 21.

5 *DA*, 19; *DE*, 13.

6 *DA*, x; *DE*, x.

7 *DA*, 91; *DE*, 84.

8 *DA*, 31; *DE*, 24.

9 *DA*, 202; *DE*, 193.
10 *KT*, **II**, 157.
11 *KT*, **I**, 117.
12 *KT*, **II**, 193.
13 *KT*, **II**, 168.
14 *KT*, **II**, 159.
15 *KT*, **II**, 159.
16 *KT*, **II**, 168.
17 *KT*, **II**, 168.
18 *KT*, **II**, 162.
19 *KT*, **II**, 162.
20 *KT*, **II**, 157.
21 *DA*, 38; *DE*, 32.
22 *DA*, 41; *DE*, 34.
23 *DA*, 43; *DE*, 36.
24 *DA*, 12; *DE*, 6–7.
25 *DA*, 36; *DE*, 29.
26 *DA*, 13; *DE*, 6–7.
27 *DA*, 15; *DE*, 9.
28 *DA*, 40; *DE*, 33.
29 *DA*, 42; *DE*, 35.
30 *DA*, 43; *DE*, 37.
31 *DA*, 42; *DE*, 36.
32 *DA*, 52; *DE*, 45–6.
33 *DA*, 6; *DE*, xvi.
34 *DA*, 41; *DE*, 34.
35 *DA*, 55 ff; *DE*, 48 ff.
36 *DA*, 57; *DE*, 50.
37 *DA*, 40; *DE*, 34.
38 *DA*, 40; *DE*, 34.
39 *DA*, 56–7; *DE*, 49–50.
40 *DA*, 59–61; *DE*, 52–3.
41 *DA*, 61; *DE*, 54.
42 *DA*, 61; *DE*, 53–4.
43 *DA*, 62; *DE*, 55.
44 *DA*, 3; *DE*, xiii.
45 *DA*, 1; *DE*, xi.
46 *Capital*, **I**, 183–4.
47 *Capital*, **III**, 795.
48 See R. Rosdolsky, 'Einige Bemerkungen über die Methode des Marxschen "Kapital" und ihre Bedeutung für die heutige Marxforschung' in W. Euchner, A. Schmidt (Hg.), *Kritik der Politishen Ökonomie heute. 100 Jahre 'Kapital'*.
49 *DA*, 38; *DE*, 31–2.
50 *DA*, 46; *DE*, 39.
51 *DA*, 46; *DE*, 39.
52 *DA*, 20; *DE*, 14.
53 *DA*, 20; *DE*, 14.
54 *DA*, 27–8; *DE*, 21.

55 See C. Taylor, 'From Marxism to the dialogue society' in T. Eagleton,
   B. Wicker (eds.), *From Culture to Revolution* (London 1968), 148–81.

Chapter Five

1 M. Horkheimer, 'Traditionelle und Kritische Theorie' in *Kritische Theorie*, **2**
   (Frankfurt 1968), 168.
2 Ibid. 170.
3 Ibid, 162.
4 H. Marcuse, 'Ist die Idee der Revolution eine Mystifikation? Herbert
   Marcuse antwortet auf vier Fragen', in *Kursbuch*, **9** (1967), 1.
5 H. Marcuse, 'Repressive Tolerance', in *A Critique of Pure Tolerance*, with
   Robert Paul Wolff and Barrington Moore, Jr (Boston 1965).
6 H. Marcuse, *Triebstruktur und Gesellschaft* (Frankfurt 1955), 12.
7 H. Marcuse, *Psychoanalyse und Politik* (Frankfurt 1968), 47.
8 H. Marcuse, *Triebstruktur und Gesellschaft* (Frankfurt 1955), 11.
9 H. Marcuse, *Das Ende der Utopie* (Berlin 1967), 61.
10 P. Sedgwick, 'Natural Science and Human Theory', *The Socialist Register*
   (1966), 169.
11 H. Marcuse, *Der eindimensionale Mensch* (Neuwied/Berlin 1967), 73.
12 H. Marcuse, 'The End of Utopia', in *Five Lectures* (London 1970), 62–82.
13 Ibid. 62–82.
14 H. Marcuse, 'Liberation from the Affluent Society' in D. Cooper, ed. *The
   Dialectics of Liberation* (London 1968), 177.
15 See J. Orr, 'German Social Theory and the Hidden Face of Technology',
   Archives européenes de sociologie, **XV** (1974), 312–36.
16 H. Marcuse, 'Der Kampf gegen den Liberalismus in der totalitären
   Staatsauffassung', in W. Abendroth, Hg., *Faschismus und Kapitalismus. Theorien
   über die sozialen Ursprünge und die Funktion des Faschismus* (Frankfurt 1967), 42.
17 Ibid.

Chapter Six

1 K. Marx and F. Engels, *Historisch-kritische Geamtausgabe* (Berlin 1932), **I**, 3,
   p. 123.
2 M. Horkheimer, *Kritische Theorie* (Frankfurt 1968), **II**, 137.
3 *KT*, **II**, 139.
4 *KT*, **II**, 144.
5 *KT*, **II**, 143.
6 See K-O. Apel, 'Communication and the Foundations of the Humanities',
   Acta Sociologica, **15** (1972), 7–26.
7 See in particular J. Habermas, 'The Classical Doctrine of Politics in Relation
   to Social Philosophy', and 'Labour and Interaction: Remarks on Hegel's
   Jena *Philosophy of Mind*' in *Theory and Practice* (London 1974), 41–81, 142–69;
   and ibid. 'Knowledge and Human Interests: A General Perspective', in
   Knowledge and Human Interests (London 1972), 301–17.
8 See J. Habermas, 'Technology and Science as "Ideology"' in *Towards a
   Rational Society* (London 1971), 87, 91–4.
9 Ibid. 92.

10 J. Habermas, *Knowledge and Human Interests* (London 1972), 308–11.
11 J. Habermas, *Toward a Rational Society* (London 1971), 100–7.
12 J. Habermas, *Theory and Practice* (London 1974), 195.
13 J. Habermas, *Toward a Rational Society* (London 1971), 102 ff.
14 J. Habermas, *Theory and Practice* (London 1974), 254.
15 J. Habermas, *Toward a Rational Society* (London 1971), 102 ff.
16 See G. Rohrmoser, *Das Elend der Kritischen Theorie* (Freiburg 1970), 97.
17 See J. Habermas, 'Towards a Theory of Communicative Competence',
     Inquiry, **13** (1970), 360–75.
18 See J. Habermas, 'On Systematically Distorted Communication', *Inquiry*, **13**
     (1970), 205–18. For a critical discussion of this aspect of Habermas' work,
     see H. J. Giegel, 'Reflexion und Emanzipation', in *Hermeneutik und
     Ideologiekritik* (Frankfurt 1971), 244–82.
19 See especially H. G. Gadamer, *Truth and Method* (London 1975).
20 See J. Habermas, *Knowledge and Human Interests* (London 1972), Chapter 10,
     and P. Ricoeur, *Freud and Philosophy; an Essay on Interpretation* (Yale 1970).
21 J. Habermas, *Knowledge and Human Interests* (London 1972), 218.
22 J. Habermas, 'Towards a Theory of Communicative Competence', *Inquiry*,
     13 (1970), 360–75.
23 J. Habermas, *Theory and Practice* (London 1974), 255.
24 Ibid. 255.
25 Ibid. 255.
26 Ibid. 255.
27 J. Habermas, *Protestbewegung und Hochschulreform* (Frankfurt 1969), 245.
28 J. Habermas, N. Luhmann, *Theorie der Gesellschaft oder Sozialtechnologie*
     (Frankfurt 1971), 266.

Chapter Seven

 1 See R. Kosellek, 'Historia magistra vitae. Über die Auflösung des Topos im
     Horizont neuzeitlich bewegter Geschichte' in H. Braun, M. Riedel, Hgg.
     Natur und Geschichte, Karl Löwith zum 70. Geburtstag (Frankfurt 1967),
     196–219.
 2 K. Marx, *Frühschriften*, ed. S. Landshut (Stuttgart 1964), 366.
 3 Ibid. 395 ff.
 4 Ibid. 246, 252, 269, 281.
 5 M. Horkheimer, *Kritische Theorie*, (Frankfurt 1968) **II**, 148–53.
 6 *Kritische Theorie*, **II**, 199.
 7 *KT*, **II**, 189.
 8 *KT*, **II**, 181.
 9 *KT*, **I**, 95.
10 *KT*, **II**, 112 ff.
11 *KT*, **II**, 116.
12 See J. Cohen, 'Critical Theory: the Philosophy of Marcuse', *New Left Review*,
     57 (1969), 35–51.
13 H. Marcuse, *Reason and Revolution* (London 1968), 295–6.
14 H. Marcuse, 'Liberation from the Affluent Society', in D. Cooper, ed. *The
     Dialectics of Liberation* (London 1968), 177.
15 T. W. Adorno, *Negative Dialektik* (Frankfurt 1966), 313.

16 T. W. Adorno, *Eingriffe* (Frankfurt 1968), 32.

17 T. W. Adorno, *Negative Dialektik* (Frankfurt 1966), 312.

18 See A. Künzli, *Aufklärung und Dialektik* (Freiburg 1971), 127 ff.

19 J. Habermas, 'Über das Subjekt der Geschichte. Kurze Bemerkungen zu falsch gestellten Alternativen', in R. Kosellek, W-D. Stempel, Hgg., *Geschichte – Ereignis und Erzählung* (München 1973), 470–6.

20 J. Habermas, 'Technology and Science as "Ideology"', in *Toward a Rational Society* (London 1971), 97–8.

21 J. Habermas, 'Über das Subjekt der Geschichte. Kurze Bemerkungen zu falsch gestellten Alternativen', in R. Kosellek, W-D. Stempel, Hgg., *Geschichte – Ereignis und Erzählung* (München 1973), 476.

22 J. Habermas, *Knowledge and Human Interests* (London 1972), 312.

23 J. Habermas, *Knowledge and Human Interests* (London 1972), 314.

24. Ibid. 314.

25 Ibid. 314.

26 Ibid. 315.

27 J. Habermas, 'Über das Subjekt der Geschichte. Kurze Bemerkungen zu falsch gestellten Alternativen', in R. Kosellek, W-D. Stempel, Hgg., *Geschichte – Ereignis und Erzählung* (München 1973), 476.

28 I. Kant, 'Beantwortung der Frage: Was ist Aufklärung?', in *Werke*, Hg. Cassirer, **IV**, 169.

29 O. Marquard, *Schwierigkeiten mit der Geschichtsphilosophie* (Frankfurt 1973), 83–106.

30 I. Kant, 'Über den Grund des Misslingens aller philosophischen Versuche in der Theodizee' (1791), in *Werke*, Hg. Cassirer, **VIII**, 255.

31 O. Marquard, *Schwierigkeiten mit der Geschichtsphilosophie* (Frankfurt 1973), 69.

32 G. Lukács, *Geschichte und Klassenbewusstsein* (Neuwied/Berlin 1967), 223.

33 K. Lenk, 'Das tragische Bewusstsein in der deutschen Soziologie' in *Marx in der Wissenssoziologie* (Neuwied/Berlin 1972) 9–42.

34 G. Simmel, 'Der Begriff und die Tragödie der Kultur', in *Philosophische Kultur* (Leipzig 1911), 245–77.

35 G. Simmel, *Lebensanschauung* (München/Leipzig 1922), 157.

36 G. Simmel, *Philosophische Kultur* (Leipzig 1911), 251.

37 Ibid, 251.

38 Ibid. 250.

39 M. Weber, 'Die Protestantische Ethik und der Geist des Kapitalismus', in *Gesammelte Aufsätze zur Religionssoziologie* (Tübingen 1920).

40 M. Weber, *Gesammelte Aufsätze zur Soziologie und Sozialpolitik* (Tübingen 1924), 412 ff.

41 M. Weber, 'Wissenschaft als Beruf', in *Gesammelte Aufsätze zur Wissenschaftslehre* (Tübingen 1922), 554.

42 Ibid. 554.

43 H. Schelsky, 'Der Mensch in der wissenschaftlichen Zivilisation', in *Auf der Suche nach Wirklichkeit* (Düsseldorf–Köln 1965), 439–80.

44 See C. Koch, D. Senghaas, Hg., *Texte zur Technokratiediskussion* (Frankfurt 1970).

45 A. Gehlen, 'Über kulturelle Kristallisation', in *Studien zur Anthropologie und Soziologie* (Neuwied/Berlin 1963), 311–28.

46 Ibid. 324.

47 Ibid. 321.

48 A. Gehlen, *Urmensch und Spätkultur* (Bonn 1956), 352.

49 A. Gehlen, 'Über kulturelle Evolutionen', in *Die Philosophie und die Frage nach dem Fortschritt* (Munchen 1964), 208 f.

50 See R. Aron, *La sociologie allemande contemporaine* (Paris 1950); G. Eisermann, 'Die deutsche Soziologie im Zeitraum von 1918–1933', *Kölner Zeitschrift*, **XI**, 1959; A. Giddens, *Capitalism and Modern Social Theory* (Cambridge 1971), 185–98; P. Honigsheim, G. Eisermann, 'Geschichte der Soziologie', in G. Eisermann, Hg., *Die Lehre von der Gesellschaft* (Stuttgart 1958); H. S. Hughes, *Consciousness and Society* (New York 1958); K. Lenk, *Marx in der Wissenssozologie* (Neuwied/Berlin 1972); D. Lindenlaub, *Richtungskämpfe im Verein für Sozialpolitik* (Wiesbaden 1967), 272–384; G. Lukács, *Die Zerstörung der Vernunft* (Neuwied/Berlin 1961), 506–76; A. von Martin, *Geist und Gesellschaft* (Frankfurt 1948); T. Parsons, 'Capitalism in recent German literature: Sombart and Weber', *Journal of Political Economy*, **36** (1928), 641–61; G. Roth, *The Social Democrats in Imperial Germany* (Englewood Cliffs 1963); Ibid. 'Das historische Verhältnis der Weberschen Soziologie zum Marxismus', *Kölner Zeitschrift*, **20** (1968), 433 ff.

51 W. Sombart, 'Ein Beitrag zur Bibliographie des Marxismus', in *Archiv für Sozialwissenschaft und Sozialpolitik*, **20** (1905), 413–30.

52 H. J. Marks, 'The Sources of Reformism in the Social Democratic Party of Germany, 1890–1914', *The Journal of Modern History*, **XI** (1939), 334–56.

53 K. Korsch, *Marxismus und Philosophie* (Leipzig 1930), 14.

54 As for instance in G. Lukács, *Die Zerstörung der Vernunft* (Neuwied/Berlin 1961), 506–76.

55 Quoted in E. Baumgarten, Hg., *Max Weber: Werk und Person* (Tübingen 1964), 554.

56 See M. Rubel, 'Premiers contacts des sociologues du XIXe siècle avec la pensée de Marx', *Cahiers internationaux de sociologie*, **31** (1961), 175–84; N. McInnes, 'Les débuts du marxisme théorique en France et en Italie (1880–1897)', *Cahiers d l'Institut de Science économique appliquée*, No. 102 (1960).

57 D. Lindenlaub, *Richtungskämpfe im Verein für Sozialpolitik* (Wiesbaden 1967), 280 ff.

58 'Gleitwort der Herausgeber', *Archiv für Sozialwissenschaft und Sozialpolitik* (1904), iv.

59 F. Naumann, 'Das Suchen nach dem Wesen des Kapitalismus', *Die Hilfe*, **17** (14 September 1911), 578 ff.

60 F. Tönnies, 'Die Anwendung der Deszendenztheorie auf Probleme der sozialen Entwicklung', in *Studien*, **1** (1925), 192.

61 F. Tönnies, 'Zur Einleitung in die Soziologie', in *Studien*, **1** (1925), 66.

62 Ibid. 66.

63 F. Tönnies, *Soziologie und Geschichte*, in *Studien*, **2**, 196.

64 Ibid. 196.

65 F. Tönnies, *Community and Association* (London 1955), 81.

66 G. Simmel, *Philosophie des Geldes* (Leipzig 1900), 495.

67 Ibid. 498.

68 Ibid. 499.

69 Ibid. 499.

70 M. Weber, *Wirtschaft und Gesellschaft* (Tübingen 1925), 552; cf. also 128, 559 ff., 570, 578, 833 ff.
71 H. Schelsky, 'Der Mensch in der wissenschaftlichen Zivilisation', in *Auf der Suche nach Wirklichkeit* (Düsseldorf–Köln 1965), 439–80.
72 Ibid. 444–5.
73 T. W. Adorno, M. Horkheimer, *Dialectic of Enlightenment*, tr. J. Cumming (London 1973), 121.
74 Ibid. 121.
75 T. W. Adorno, 'Einleitungsvortrag zum 16. deutschen Soziologentag' in *Spätkapitalismus oder Industriegesellschaft?* Hg. T. W. Adorno (Stuttgart 1969), 12–28.
76 T. W. Adorno, *Negative Dialektik* (Frankfurt 1966), 137 ff.; see also K. H. Haag, 'Das Unwiederholbare' in *Philosophischer Idealismus* (Frankfurt 1967), 5–17.
77 T. W. Adorno, M. Horkheimer, *Dialectic of Enlightenment*, 7.
78 H. Marcuse, *Der eindimensionale Mensch* (Neuwied/Berlin 1967), 73.
79 Ibid. 69.
80 See C. Offe, 'Technik und Eindimensionalität. Eine Version der Technokratiethese?', in J. Habermas, Hg., *Antworten auf Herbert Marcuse* (Frankfurt 1968), 73–88.
81 See especially H. Marcuse, *Der eindimensionale Mensch*, 159–83.
82 H. Marcuse, 'Industrialization and Capitalism in the Work of Max Weber', in *Negations* (London 1968), 223–4.
83 J. Habermas, *Toward a Rational Society* (London 1971), 64.
84 J. Habermas, *Legitimationsprobleme im Spätkapitalismus* (Frankfurt 1973).
85 J. Habermas, *Theory and Practice* (London 1974), 195.
86 J. Habermas, *Toward a Rational Society* (London 1971), 108.
87 J. Habermas, *Knowledge and Human Interests* (London 1972), esp. 301–17.
88 For a critique of this position see N. Lobkowicz, 'Interest and Objectivity', *Philosophy of the Social Sciences*, No. 2 (1972), 193–210.

Chapter Eight

1 T. W. Adorno, *Minima Moralia* (Frankfurt 1951), 11.
2 M. Horkheimer. 'Theismus-Atheismus', in *Zeugnisse* (Frankfurt 1962).
3 M. Horkheimer, *Kritische Theorie* (Frankfurt 1968), I, xii.
4 H. Marcuse, *Kultur und Gesellschaft*, 1 (Frankfurt 1968), 7.
5 J. Habermas, *Knowledge and Human Interests*, (London 1972), 302.
6 H. Böhme, *Deutschlands Weg zur Grossmacht. Studien zum Verhältnis von Wirtschaft und Staat während der Reichsgründungszeit 1848 bis 1881* (Köln/Berlin 1966). See J. Hirsch, *Wissenschaftlich-technischer Fortschritt und politisches System* (Frankfurt 1970), esp. 11–40.
7 See F. Lütge, *Deutsche Sozial- und Wirtschaftsgeschichte* (Berlin-Göttingen-Heidelberg 1960), 471 ff.

BIBLIOGRAPHY

Primary works

Th. W. Adorno, *Gesammelte Schriften*, G. Adorno and R. Tiedemann (eds.), 1–
    (Frankfurt 1971–)
– 'Contemporary German Sociology', *Transactions of the Fourth World Congress of
    Sociology* (1959)
– 'New Music and the Public: Some Problems of Interpretation', in R. H. Myers
    (ed.), *Twentieth Century Music* (London 1960)
– 'Sociology and Psychology', *New Left Review*, **46–7** (1966–7)
– *Prisms*, trans. S. and S. Weber (London 1967)
– 'Scientific Experiences of a European Scholar in America', in D. Fleming and
    B. Bailyn (eds.), *The Intellectual Migration. Europe and America 1930–1960*
    (Cambridge, Mass. 1969)
– 'Society', *Salmagundi*, **10/11** (1969–70)
– 'Theses on the Sociology of Art', *Birmingham Cultural Studies*, **2** (1972)
– *Jargon of Authenticity*, trans, K. Tarnowski and F. Will (London 1973)
– *Negative Dialectics*, trans. E. B. Ashton (London 1973)
– 'Letters to Walter Benjamin', *New Left Review*, **81** (1973)
– 'Commitment', *New Left Review*, **87/8** (1974)
– *Minima Moralia*, trans. E. F. N. Jephcott (London 1974)
– 'Lyric Poetry and Society', *Telos*, **20** (1974)
– *'The Positivist Dispute in German Sociology'*, trans, G. Adey and D. Frisby
    (London 1976)
– 'Culture Industry Reconsidered', *New German Critique*, **6** (1975)
– 'The Actuality of Philosophy', *Telos*, **31** (1977)
– 'Music and Technique', *Telos*, **32** (1977)
J. Habermas (*et al.*), *Student und Politik* (Frankfurt 1961)
– *Strukturwandel der Öffentlichkeit* (Frankfurt 1962)
– *Theorie und Praxis* (Frankfurt 1963)
– *Technik und Wissenschaft als 'Ideologie'* (Frankfurt 1968)
– *Erkenntnis und Interesse* (Frankfurt 1968)
– *Protestbewegung und Hochschulreform* (Frankfurt 1969)
– *Zur Logik der Sozialwissenschaften* (Frankfurt 1970)
– *Arbeit, Erkenntnis, Fortschritt* (Amsterdam 1970)

- *Philosophisch-politische Profile* (Frankfurt 1971)
- 'Der Universalitätsanspruch der Hermeneutik', in *Hermeneutik und Ideologiekritik* (Frankfurt 1971)
- (with N. Luhmann), *Theorie der Gesellschaft oder Sozialtechnologie* (Frankfurt 1971)
- *Legitimationsprobleme im Spätkapitalismus* (Frankfurt 1973)
- *Kultur und Kritik* (Frankfurt 1973)
- (with D. Henrich), *Zwei Reden* (Frankfurt 1974)
- *Zur Rekonstruktion des Historischen Materialismus* (Frankfurt 1976)
- 'Einige Bemerkungen zum Problem der Begründung von Werturteilen', *9. Deutscher Kongress fur Philosophie, Dusseldorf* (1969)
- 'Wahrheitstheorien', in *Wirklichkeit und Reflexion: Walter Schulz zum 60 Geburtstag* (Pfüllingen 1973)
- 'Sprachspiel, Intention und Bedeutung: zum Motiven bei Sellars und Wittgenstein', in R. Wiggerhaus (ed.), *Sprachanalyse und Soziologie* (Frankfurt 1975)
- 'Was heisst Universalpragmatik', in K-O. Apel (ed.), *Sprachpragmatik und Philosophie* (Frankfurt 1976)
- 'Universalpragmatische Hinweise auf das System der Ich-Abgrenzungen', in M. Auswarter, E. Kirsch and K. Schroter (eds.), *Seminar: Kommunikation, Interaktion, Identität* (Frankfurt 1976)
- 'Antwort' to critical remarks by H. Girndt and E. Simons, in P. Kielmansegg (ed.), 'Legitimationsprobleme politischer Systeme, Sonderheft 7 (1976), *Politische Viertenjahresschrift*
- *Toward a Rational Society*, trans. J. Shapiro (London 1970)
- *Knowledge and Human Interests*, trans. J. Shapiro (London 1971)
- *Theorie und Praxis*, trans. J. Viertel (London 1973)
- *Legitimation Crisis in Late Capitalism*, trans. T. A. McCarthy (London 1975)
- 'Ernst Bloch – A Marxist Romantic', *Salmagundi*, **10/11** (1969/70)
- 'Towards a Theory of Communicative Competence', *Inquiry*, **13** (1970)
- 'Summation and Response', *Continuum*, **8** (1970)
- 'On Systematically Distorted Communication', *Inquiry*, **13** (1970)
- 'Towards a Theory of Communicative Competence', *Inquiry*, **13** (1970)
- 'Why More Philosophy?' *Social Research*, **38** (1971)
- 'What Does a Crisis Mean Today? Legitimation Problems in Late Capitalism', *Social Research*, **40** (1973)
- 'On Social Identity', *Telos*, **19** (1974)
- 'The Public Sphere', *New German Critique*, **3** (1974)
- 'A Postscript to "Knowledge and Human Interests"', *Philosophy of the Social Sciences*, **3** (1975)
- 'Towards a Reconstruction of Historical Materialism', *Theory and Society*, **2** (1975)
- 'Moral Development and Ego Identity', *Telos*, **24** (1975)
- 'Moral Development and Ego Identity: A Clarification', *Telos*, **27** (1976)
- 'Some Distinctions in Universal Pragmatics', *Theory and Society*, **3** (1976)
- 'The Analytical Theory of Science and Dialectics', in Th. W. Adorno et al., *The Positivist Dispute in German Sociology* (London 1976)
- 'A Positivistically Bisected Rationalism', in Th. W. Adorno et al., *The Positivist Dispute in German Sociology* (London 1976)

M. Horkheimer, *Über Kants Kritik der Urteilskraft als Bindeglied zwischen theoretischer und praktischer Philosophie* (Stuttgart 1925)
– (ed.), *Studien über Autorität und Familie* (Paris 1936)
– *Eclipse of Reason* (London 1947)
– (ed.), *Studies in Prejudice* (New York 1949–50)
– (ed.), *Zeugnisse. Theodor W. Adorno zum sechzigsten Geburtstag* (Frankfurt 1963)
– *Zur Kritik der instrumentellen Vernunft* (Frankfurt 1967)
– *Kritische Theorie*, 2 Vols. A. Schmidt (ed.) (Frankfurt 1968)
– *Verwaltete Welt? Ein Gespräch* (Zurich 1970)
– *Vernunft und Selbsterhaltung* (Frankfurt 1970)
– *Anfänge der bürgerlichen Geschichtsphilosophie* (Frankfurt 1971)
– *Sozialphilosophische Studien*, W. Brede (ed.) (Frankfurt 1972)
– *Notizen 1950–1969 und Dämmerung* (Frankfurt 1974)
– *Critical Theory. Selected Essays*, trans. M. J. O'Connell and others (New York 1972)
M. Horkheimer and Th. W. Adorno, *Dialektik der Aufklärung* (Frankfurt 1969)
– *Dialectic of Enlightenment*, trans. J. Cumming (New York 1972)
– *Aspects of Sociology*, trans. J. Viertel (London 1973)
H. Marcuse, *Eros and Civilization* (Boston 1955)
– *One-Dimensional Man* (London 1964)
– *Kultur und Gesellschaft*, 2 Vols. (Frankfurt 1965)
– 'On Science and Phenomenology', *Boston Studies in the Philosophy of Science*, **2** (1965)
– (with R. P. Wolff and Barrington Moore Jr), *A Critique of Pure Tolerance* (Boston 1965)
– 'The Obsolescence of Marxism', in N. Lobkowicz (ed.), *Marx and the Western World* (Notre Dame 1967)
– *Negations* (London 1968)
– *Soviet Marxism* (London 1968)
– *Reason and Revolution. Hegel and the Rise of Social Theory* (London 1968)
– *Hegels Ontologie und die Theorie der Geschichtlichkeit* (Frankfurt 1968)
– *Ideen zu einer Kritischen Theorie der Gesellschaft* (Frankfurt 1969)
– *An Essay on Liberation* (London 1969)
– *Five Lectures* (London 1970)
– *Studies in Critical Philosophy* (London 1972)
– *Counter-revolution and Revolt* (Boston 1973)
Zeitschrift für Sozialforschung (München 1970)

Secondary works

H. Albert, *Traktat über kritische Vernunft* (Tübingen 1969)
– *Plädoyer für kritischen Rationalismus* (München 1971)
– *Konstruktion und Kritik. Aufsätze zur Philosophie des kritischen Rationalismus* (Hamburg 1972)
L. Althusser and E. Balibar, *Reading Capital*, trans, B. Brewster (London 1971)
R. Altmann, 'Brüder im Nichts? Zur Auseinandersetzung Jürgen Habermas mit Arnold Gehlen', *Merkur*, **266** (1970)
P. Anderson, *Considerations on Western Marxism* (London 1976)
K-O. Apel, 'Das "Verstehen" – eine Problemgeschichte als Begriffsgeschichte', *Archiv für Begriffsgeschichte*, **1** (1955)

- 'Reflexion und materielle Praxis', *Hegel-Studien*, Beiheft **1** (1964)
- *Analytical Philosophy of Language and the Geisteswissenschaften* (Dordrecht 1969)
- 'Wissenschaft als Emanzipation?', *Zeitschrift fur allgemeine Wissenschaftstheorie*, **1** (1970)
- 'Szientistik, Hermeneutik, Ideologiekritik. Entwurf einer Wissenschaftslehre in erkenntnisanthropologischer Sicht', in *Hermeneutik und Ideologiekritik* (Frankfurt 1971)
- 'Communication and the Foundations of the Humanities', *Acta Sociologica*, **15** (1972)
- *Transformation der Philosophie*, 2 Vols. (Frankfurt 1973)
- A. Arato, 'Lukacs' Theory of Reification', *Telos*, **2** (1972)
- H. Arendt, *The Human Condition* (London 1958)
- J. P. Arnanson, *Von Marcuse zu Marx* (Frankfurt 1971)
- R. Aron, *German Sociology*, trans. M. and T. Bottomore (London 1957)
- *Main Currents in Sociological Thought*, 2 Vols. (Harmondsworth 1968)
- K. Axelos, 'Adorno et l'école de Francfort', *Arguments*, **111** (1959)
- H. D. Bahr, *Kritik der 'Politischen Technologie'* (Frankfurt 1970)
- H. Baier, 'Soziologie und Geschichte', *Archiv für Rechts- und Sozialphilosophie*, **52** (1966)
- 'Soziale Technologie oder soziale Emanzipation?' in B. Schäfers (ed.) *Thesen zur Kritik der Soziologie* (Frankfurt 1969)
- K. Ballestram and T. A. McCarthy, 'Thesen zür Begrundung einer Kritischen Theorie der Gesellschaft', *Zeitschrift für allgemeine Wissenschaftstheorie*, **3** (1972)
- Z. Bauman, *Towards a Critical Sociology* (London 1976)
- H. M. Baumgartner, *Kontinuität und Geschichte* (Frankfurt 1972)
- J. Berger, 'Historische Logik und Hermeneutik', *Philosophisches Jahrbuch*, **75** (1967)
- P. Berger and S. Pullberg, 'Reification and the Sociological Critique of Consciousness', *History and Theory*, **IV** (1965)
- R. J. Bernstein, *The Restructuring of Social and Political Theory* (New York 1976)
- E. Betti, 'Zur Grundlegung einer allgemeinen Auslegungslehre', in *Festschrift für E. Rabel*, Vol. 2 (Tübingen 1954)
- *Die Hermeneutik als allgemeine Methodik des Geisteswissenschaften* (Tübingen 1962)
- R. W. Beyer, *Vier Kritiker: Heidegger, Sartre, Adorno, Lukács* (Köln 1970)
- N. Birnbaum, *Towards a Critical Sociology* (New York 1971)
- W. V. Bloomster, 'Sociology of Music: Adorno and Beyond', *Telos*, **28** (1976)
- H. Blumenberg, *Die Legitimität der Neuzeit* (Frankfurt 1966)
- F. Bockelmann, *Über Marx und Adorno* (Frankfurt 1972)
- D. Böhler, 'Das Problem des "emanzipatorischen Interesses" und seine gesellschaftlichen Wahrnehmung', *Man and World*, **3** (1970)
- *Metakritik der Marxschen Ideologiekritik* (Frankfurt 1971)
- K. Böhmer, 'Adorno, Musik, Gesellschaft', in W. F. Schöller (ed.) *Die neue Linke nach Adorno* (München 1969)
- C. Bormann, 'Die Zweideutigkeit der hermeneutischen Erfahrung', in *Hermeneutik und Ideologiekritik* (Frankfurt 1971), 83–119
- P. Breines (ed.), *Critical Interruptions: New Perspectives on Herbert Marcuse* (New York 1970)
- H. Brenner, 'Theodor Adorno als Sachwalter des Benjaminschen Werkes', in W. F. Schöller (ed.) *Die neue Linke nach Adorno* (München 1969)

M. von Brentano, 'Die unbescheidene Philosophie. Der Streit um die Theorie der Sozialwissenschaften', *Das Argument*, **9** (1967)

R. Bubner, K. Cramer and R. Wiehl (eds.) *Hermeneutik und Dialektik,* 2 Vols. (Tübingen 1970)

R. Bubner, 'Was ist kritische Theorie', in *Hermeneutik und Ideologiekritik* (Frankfurt 1971), 160–209

R. Christie and M. Jahoda (eds.), *Studies in the Scope and Method of 'The Authoritarian Personality'* (Glencoe 1954)

D. Claussen, 'Zum emanzipativen Gehalt der materialistischen Dialektik in Horkheimers Konzeption der kritischen Theorie', *Neue Kritik*, **55/56** (1970)

M. Clemenz, 'Theorie als Praxis', *Neue Politische Literatur*, **XIII** (1968)

J. Cohen, 'Critical Theory: The Philosophy of Marcuse', *New Left Review*, **57** (1969)

L. Colletti, *From Rousseau to Lenin* (London 1972)

P. Connerton (ed.), *Critical Sociology* (Harmondsworth 1976)

H. Dahmer, 'Psychoanalyse und historischer Materialismus', in *Psychoanalyse als Sozialwissenschaft* (Frankfurt 1971), 60–92

R. Dahrendorf, *Society and Democracy in Germany* (London 1968)

F. Dallmayr, 'Habermas: Knowledge and Human Interests and its Aftermath', *Philosophy of the Social Sciences*, **3** (1972)

– 'Reason and Emancipation', *Man and World*, **5** (1972)

– 'Phenomenology and Critical Theory', *Cultural Hermeneutics*, **3** (1975/6)

W. Dilthey, *Der Aufbau der geschichtlichen Welt in den Geisteswissenschaften.* Einleitung von M. Riedel (Frankfurt 1970)

H. P. Dreitzel (ed.), *Recent sociology No. 2. Patterns of Communicative Behaviour* (London 1970)

H. Dubiel, 'Dialektische Wissenschaftskritik und interdisziplinäre Sozialforschung. Theorie und Organisationsstruktur des Frankfurter Instituts für Sozialforschung', *Kölner Zeitschrift fur Soziologie und Sozialpsychologie*, **XXVI** (1974)

G. Eisermann, 'Die deutsche Soziologie im Zeitraum von 1918–1933' *Kölner Zeitschrift fur Soziologie und Sozialpsychologie*, **XI** (1959)

W. Euchner and A. Schmidt (eds.), *Kritik der Politischen Ökonomie heute. 100 Jahre Kapital* (Frankfurt 1968)

B. Fay, *Social Theory and Political Practice* (London 1975)

A. Feenberg, 'Reification and the Antinomies of Socialist Thought', *Telos*, **10** (1971)

H. Fleischer, *Marxism and History*, trans. E. Mosbacher (London 1973)

E. Fleischmann, 'De Weber à Nietzsche', *European Journal of Sociology*, **V** (1964)

– 'Fin de la sociologie dialectique?' *European Journal of Sociology*, **XIV** (1973)

G. Floistadt, 'Social Concepts of Action: notes on Habermas' Proposal for a Social Theory of Action', *Inquiry*, **13** (1970)

Folgen einer Theorie. Essays uber 'Das Kapital' von Karl Marx, (Frankfurt 1967)

I. Frenzel, 'Zur Kritischen Theorie Max Horkheimers, *Neue Rundschau*, **80** (1969)

D. Frisby, 'The Popper–Adorno Controversy: the Methodological Dispute in German Sociology', *Philosophy of the Social Sciences*, **2** (1972)

H-G. Gadamer, *Wahrheit und Methode* (Tübingen 1965)

– *Kleine Schriften*, 4 Vols. (Tübingen 1967–77)

P. Gay, *Weimar Culture: The Outsider as Insider* (New York 1968)

A. Gehlen, 'Über kulturelle Kristallisation', in *Studien zur Anthropologie und Soziologie* (Neuwied/Berlin 1963)

– 'Über kulturelle Evolutionen', in *Die Philosophie und die Frage nach dem Fortschritt* (München 1964)

A. Giddens, *Capitalism and Modern Social Theory* (Cambridge 1971)

– *Positivism and Sociology* (London 1974)

– *Studies in Social and Political Theory* (London 1977)

H.-J. Giegel, 'Reflexion und Emanzipation', in *Hermeneutik und Ideologiekritik* (Frankfurt 1971), 244–82

L. Goldmann, *Recherches dialectiques* (Paris 1959)

– 'La pensée de Herbert Marcuse', *La Nef*, **36** (1969)

F. Grenz, *Adornos Philosophie in Grundbegriffen* (Frankfurt 1974)

P. Hamilton, *Knowledge and Social Structure* (London 1974)

K. Hartmann, *Die Marxsche Theorie. Eine philosophische Untersuchung zu den Hauptschriften* (Berlin 1970)

W. F. Haug, 'Sexuelle Verschwörung des Spätkapitalismus', *Neue Kritik*, **51/52** (1969)

J. H. Heiseler, R. Steigerwald and J. Schleiftstein (eds.), *Die 'Frankfurter Schule' im Lichte des Marxismus* (Frankfurt 1970)

W. Hennis, 'Ende der Politik? Zur Krisis der Politik in der Neuzeit', *Merkur*, **278** (1971)

E. Hirsch, *Validity in Interpretation* (New Haven 1967)

– 'Three Dimensions of Hermeneutics', *New Literary History*, **111** (1972)

J. Hirsch, *Wissenschaftlich-technischer Fortschritt und politisches System* (Frankfurt 1970)

H. H. Holz, *Utopie und Anarchismus. Zur Kritik der Kritischen Theorie Herbert Marcuses* (Köln 1968)

H. Holzer, *Gescheiterte Aufklärung? Politik, Ökonomie und Kommunikation in der Bundesrepublik Deutschlands* (München 1971)

H. Holzhey, 'Psychoanalyse und Gesellschaft', *Psyche*, **3** (1970)

D. Howard and K. Clare (eds.), *The Unknown Dimension: European Marxism since Lenin* (New York 1972)

K. J. Huch, 'Interesse an Emanzipation', *Neue Rundschau*, **80** (1969)

H. S. Hughes, *Consciousness and Society* (New York 1968)

M. Jablinski, *Theodor W. Adorno. Kritische Theorie der Literatur – und Kunstkritik* (Bonn 1976)

U. Jaeggi, 'Developmental Interaction between American and German Sociology', *Social Research*, **43** (1976)

W. Jager, *Öffentlichkeit und Parlamentarismus. Eine Kritik an Jürgen Habermas* (Stuttgart, Berlin, Koln, Mainz 1973)

F. Jameson, *Marxism and Form; Twentieth-Century Dialectical Theories of Literature* (Princeton 1971)

H. Janson, *Herbert Marcuse* (Bonn 1971)

M. Jay, 'The Metapolitics of Utopianism', *Dissent*, **XVII** (1970)

– 'The Frankfurt School in Exile', *Perspectives in American History*, **VI** (Cambridge, Mass. 1972)

– 'The Frankfurt School's Critique of Marxist Humanism', *Social Research*, **XXXIX** (1972)

156 *The tragedy of enlightenment*

- *The Dialectical Imagination. A History of the Frankfurt School and the Institute of Social Research 1923–1950* (Boston 1973)
- 'The Frankfurt School's Critique of Karl Mannheim and the Sociology of Knowledge', *Telos*, **20** (1974)
- 'The Concept of Totality in Lukács and Adorno', *Telos*, **32** (1977)

G. Stedman Jones et al., *Western Marxism. A Critical Reader* (London 1977)

G. Kaiser, *Benjamin, Adorno. Zwei Studien* (Frankfurt 1974)

H. Kimmerle, 'Hermeneutische Theorie oder ontologische Hermeneutik', *Zeitschrift für Theologie und Kirche*, **59** (1962)
- 'Metahermeneutik, Applikation, hermeneutische Sprachbildung', *Zeitschrift für Theologie und Kirche*, **61** (1964)
- 'Die Funktion der Hermeneutik in den positiven Wissenschaften', *Zeitschrift für allgemeine Wissenschaftstheorie*, **5** (1974)

A. Klüge, O. Negt, *Öffentlichkeit und Erfahrung. Zur Organisationsanalyse von bürgerlicher und proletarischer Öffentlichkeit* (Frankfurt 1973)

C. Koch and D. Senghaas (eds.), *Texte zur Technokratiediskussion* (Frankfurt 1970)

A. Kohli-Kunz, *Erinnern und Vergessen* (Berlin 1973)

L. Kolakowski, *Positivist Philosophy* (London 1972)

K. Korsch, *Marxism and Philosophy*, trans. F. Halliday (London 1970)

R. Kosellek, *Kritik und Krise* (Freiburg, München 1959)
- 'Historia magistra vitae. Über die Auflösung des Topos im Horizont neuzeitlich bewegter Geschichte', in H. Braun, M. Riedel (eds.), *Natur und Geschichte. Karl Lowith zum 70. Geburtstag* (Frankfurt 1967), 196–219

H.-J. Krahl, *Konstitution und Klassenkampf. Zur historischen Dialektik von bürgerlicher Emanzipation und proletarischer Revolution* (Frankfurt 1971)
- 'The Political Contradiction in Adorno's Critical Theory', *Telos*, **21** (1974)

W. Kunstmann, *Gesellschaft, Emanzipation, Diskurs. Darstellung und Kritik der Gesellschaftstheorie von Jürgen Habermas* (München 1977)

A. Künzli, *Aufklärung und Dialektik* (Freiburg 1971)

J. Laplanche, 'Notes sur Marcuse et la Psychoanalyse', *La Nef*, **36** (1969)

W. Leiss, *The Domination of Nature* (New York 1972)

C. K. Lenhardt, 'Rise and Fall of Transcendental Anthropology', *Philosophy of the Social Sciences*, **2** (1972)

K. Lenk, *Marx in der Wissenssoziologie* (Neuwied/Berlin 1972)

W. Lepenies, 'Anthropology and Social Criticism: A View on the Controversy between Arnold Gehlen and Jürgen Habermas', *The Human Context*, **3** (1971)

H. Ley and Th. Müller, *Kritische Vernunft und Revolution. Zur Kontroverse zwischen Hans Albert und Jürgen Habermas* (Köln 1971)

G. Lichtheim, *Lukács* (London 1970)
- *From Marx to Hegel* (London 1971)

D. Lindenlaub, *Richtungskämpfe im Verein für Sozialpolitik* (Wiesbaden 1967)

W. Lipp, 'Apparat und Gewalt', *Soziale Welt*, **20** (1970)

N. Lobkowicz, *Theory and Practice: The History of a Concept* (Notre Dame 1967)
- 'Interest and Objectivity', *Philosophy of the Social Sciences*, **2** (1972)

A. Lorenzer, *Kritik des psychoanalytischen Symbolbegriffs* (Frankfurt 1970)
- *Sprachzerstörung und Rekonstruktion* (Frankfurt 1970)
- 'Symbol, Interaktion, und Praxis', in *Psychoanalyse als Sozialwissenschaft* (Frankfurt 1971), 9–59

G. Lukács, *Die Zerstörung der Vernunft* (Neuwied/Berlin 1961)

– *History and Class Consciousness*, trans. R. Livingstone (London 1971)

N. Luhmann, 'Öffentliche Meinung', *Politische Vierteljahresschrift*, **11** (1970)

F. Lütge, *Deutsche Sozial- und Wirtschaftsgeschichte* (Berlin, Göttingen, Heidelberg 1960)

T. A. McCarthy, *The Critical Theory of Jürgen Habermas* (London 1978)

N. McInnes, *The Western Marxists* (London 1972)

A. McIntyre, *Marcuse* (London 1970)

O. Marquard, *Schwierigkeiten mit der Geschichtsphilosophie* (Frankfurt 1973)

O. Massing, *Adorno und die Folgen. Über das 'Hermetische Prinzip' der kritischen Theorie* (Neuwied/Berlin 1970)

J. Matzner, 'Der Begriff der Charaktermaske bei Marx', *Soziale Welt*, **15** (1964)

R. K. Maurer, 'Jürgen Habermas' Aufhebung der Philosophie', *Philosophische Rundschau*, **24**, Beiheft 8 (1977)

G. Mende and E. Lange (eds.), *Die aktuelle philosophische Bedeutung des 'Kapital'* (Berlin 1968)

A. and M. Mitscherlich, *Die Unfähigkeit zu trauern* (München 1967)

A. Mitzman, *Sociology and Estrangement. Three Sociologists of Imperial Germany* (New York 1973)

O. Negt (ed.), *Die Linke antwortet Jürgen Habermas* (Frankfurt 1968)

– *Politik als Protest* (Frankfurt 1971)

C. Offe, *Strukturprobleme des kapitalistischen Staates* (Frankfurt 1972)

B. Ollman, *Alienation: Marx's Conception of Man in Capitalist Society* (London 1971)

J. O'Neill (ed.), *On Critical Theory* (London 1972)

J. Orr, 'German Social Theory and the Hidden Face of Technology', *European Journal of Sociology*, **XV** (1974)

E. Otto, 'Die Applikation als Problem der politischen Hermeneutik', *Zeitschrift für Theologie und Kirche*, **71** (1974)

K. Ottomeyer, *Soziales Verhalten und Ökonomie im Kapitalismus. Vorüberlegungen zur systematischen Vermittlung von Interaktionstheorie und Kritik der Politischen Ökonomie* (Giessen 1976)

H. Paetzold, *Neomarxistische Asthetik*, 2 Vols. (Düsseldorf 1974)

R. E. Palmer, *Hermeneutics; interpretation theory in Schleirmacher, Dilthey, Heidegger and Gadamer* (Evanston 1969)

W. Pannenberg, 'Hermeneutik und Universalgeschichte', *Zeitschrift für Theologie und Kirche*, **60** (1963)

R. Piccone and A. Delfini, 'Marcuse's Heideggerian Marxism', *Telos*, **6** (1970)

G. Picht, 'Der Sinn der Unterscheidung von Theorie und Praxis in der griechischen Philosophie', *Zeitschrift für evangelische Ethik*, **VIII** (1964)

– 'Was heisst aufgeklärtes Denken?', *Zeitschrift für evangelische Ethik*, **XI** (1967)

K. R. Popper, 'Reason or Revolution', *European Journal of Sociology*, **XI** (1970)

W. Post, *Kritische Theorie und metaphysischer Pessimismus. Zum Spätwerk Max Horkheimers* (München 1970)

P. Putz, 'Nietzsche im Licht der Kritischen Theorie', *Nietzsche Studium*, **3** (1974)

A. Quinton, 'Critical Theory', *Encounter* (1974)

G. Radnitzky, *Contemporary Schools of Metascience*, **2** (New York 1968)

R. Reiche, *Sexualität und Klassenkampf. Zur Abwehr repressiver Entsublimierung* (Frankfurt 1968)

B. W. Reimann, 'Therapie und Diskurs. Zur Problematik von Analogieschlüssen', *Soziale Welt*, **26** (1975)

J. Rex (ed.), *Approaches to Sociology* (London 1974)

P. Ricoeur, *Freud and Philosophy. An Essay on Interpretation*, trans. D. Savage (New Haven 1970)

- 'The Model of the Text: Meaningful Action Considered as a Text', *Social Research*, **38** (1971)
- 'The Hermeneutical Function of Distanciation', *Philosophy Today*, **17** (1973)
- 'Ethics and Culture: Habermas and Gadamer in Dialogue', in Ibid. *Political and Social Essays*, D. Stewart and J. Bien (eds.) (Athens 1974)

F. Ringer, *The Decline of the German Mandarins. The German Academic Community 1890–1933* (Cambridge, Mass. 1969)

J. Ritsert and C. Rolshausen, *Der Konservatismus der kritischen Theorie* (Frankfurt 1971)

J. Ritter (ed.), *Historisches Wörterbuch der Philosophie, A-K* (Darmstadt 1971–)

G. Rohrmoser, *Das Elend der kritischen Theorie* (Freiburg 1969)

G. Rose, *The Melancholy Science. An Introduction to the Thought of Theodor W. Adorno* (London 1978)

G. Roth, *The Social Democrats in Imperial Germany* (Englewood Cliffs 1963)

- 'Das historische Verhältnis der Weberschen Soziologie zum Marxismus', *Kolner Zeitschrift fur Soziologie und Sozialpsychologie*, **XX** (1968)

G. Röttgers, *Kritik und Praxis* (Berlin 1975)

P. A Rovatti, 'Fetishism and Economic Categories', *Telos*, **14** (1972)

M. Rubel, 'Premiers contacts des sociologues du XIXe siècle avec la pensée de Marx', *Cahiers internationaux de sociologie*, **31** (1961)

G. E. Rusconi, *La Teoria Critica della Società* (Bologna 1968)

H. J. Sandkühler, *Psychoanalyse und Marxismus* (Frankfurt 1970)

- *Praxis und Geschichtsbewusstsein. Fragen einer dialektischen und historisch-materialistischen Hermeneutik* (Frankfurt 1972)

A. Schaff, *Geschichte und Wahrheit* (Frankfurt 1970)

H. Schelsky, *Ortsbestimmung der deutschen Soziologie* (Dusseldorf 1959)

- 'Der Mensch in der wissenschaftlichen Zivilisation', in *Auf der Suche nach Wirklichkeit* (Dusseldorf-Köln 1965), 439–80

E. Shils, 'Daydreams and Nightmares: Reflections on the Criticism of Mass Culture', *Sewanee Review*, **LXV** (1957)

- 'Tradition, Ecology, and Institution in the History of Sociology', *Daedalus*, **LXXXIX** (1970)

A. Schmidt, 'Über Geschichte und Geschichtsschreibung in der materialistischen Dialektik', in *Folgen einer Theorie* (Frankfurt 1967), 103–29

- (ed.) *Beiträge einer marxistischen Erkenntnistheorie* (Frankfurt 1969)
- *The Concept of Nature in Marx*, trans. B. Fowkes (London 1971)
- *Geschichte und Struktur. Fragen einer marxistischen Historik* (München 1971)
- *Zur Idee der Kritischen Theorie* (München 1974)
- *Die Kritische Theorie als Geschichtsphilosophie* (München 1976)

F. W. Schmidt, 'Hegel in der Kritischen Theorie der Frankfurter Schule', in O. Negt (ed.), *Aktualität und Folgen der Philosophie Hegels* (Frankfurt 1970)

H. Schnädelbach, *Erfahrung, Begründung und Reflexion. Versuch über den Positivismus* (Frankfurt 1971)

T. Schroyer, 'The Politics of Epistemology: A Marxist Perspective on the Current Debates in German Sociology', *International Journal of Sociology*, **1** (1971–2)

– *The Critique of Domination* (New York 1973)

H. Schweppenhäuser (ed.), *Theodor W. Adorno zum Gedächtnis* (Frankfurt 1971)

– *Tractanda. Beiträge zur Kritischen Theorie der Kultur und Gesellschaft* (Frankfurt 1972)

P. Sedgwick, 'Natural Science and Human Theory', *The Socialist Register* (1966)

T. Seebohm, *Zur Kritik der hermeneutischen Vernunft* (Bonn 1972)

G. Simmel, *Philosophie des Geldes* (Leipzig 1900)

– 'Der Begriff und die Tragödie der Kultur', in *Philosophische Kultur* (Leipzig 1911), 245–77

R. Simon-Schäfer and W. Zimmerli, *Theorie zwischen Kritik und Praxis. Jürgen Habermas und die Frankfurter Schule* (Stuttgart-Bad Cannstatt 1975)

P. Slater, *Origin and Significance of the Frankfurt School. A Marxist Perspective* (London 1977)

Z. Tar, *The Frankfurt School. The Critical Theories of Max Horkheimer and Th. W. Adorno* (New York, London 1977)

C. Taylor, 'From marxism to the dialogue society', in T. Eagleton and B. Wicker (eds.), *From Culture to Revolution* (London 1968), 148–81

– 'Interpretation and the Science of Man', *Review of Metaphysics*, **25** (1971)

G. Therborn, 'Frankfurt Marxism: A Critique', *New Left Review*, **63** (1970)

– 'Jürgen Habermas: A New Eclectic', *New Left Review*, **67** (1971)

M. Theunissen, *Gesellschaft und Geschichte. Zur Kritik der Kritischen Theorie* (Berlin 1969)

– 'Die Verwirklichung der Vernunft. Zur Theorie-Praxis-Diskussion im Anschluss an Hegel', *Philosophisches Rundschau*, Beiheft 6 (1970)

R. Tiedemann, *Studien zur Philosophie Walter Benjamins* (Frankfurt 1973)

F. Tönnies, *Community and Association*, trans. C. P. Loomis (London 1955)

B. Tuschling, *Die 'offene' und die 'abstrakte' Gesellschaft. Habermas und die Konzeption von Vergesellschaftung der klassisch-bürgerlichen Rechts-und Staatsphilosophie, Das Argument*, Sonderband (Berlin 1978)

Über Theodor W. Adorno (Frankfurt 1968)

S. Unseld (ed.), *Zur Aktualität Walter Benjamins* (Frankfurt 1972)

M. Vacatello, *Th. W. Adorno: il rinvio della prassi* (Firenze 1972)

Verhandlungen des 16. Deutschen Soziologentages. Spätkapitalismus oder Industriegesellschaft (Stuttgart 1969)

J-M. Vincent, *Fétichisme et Société* (Paris 1973)

M. Weber, *Gesammelte Aufsätze zur Religionssoziologie* (Tübingen 1920)

– *Gesammelte Aufsätze zur Wissenschaftslehre* (Tübingen 1922)

A. Wellmer, *The Critical Theory of Society*, trans. J. Cumming (New York 1971)

A. Wilden, 'Marcuse and the Freudian Model: Energy, Information, and Phantasie', *Salmagundi*, **10/11** (1969/70)

B. Willms, *Kritik und Politik. Jürgen Habermas oder das politische Defizit der 'Kritischen Theorie'* (Frankfurt 1973)

K. H. Wolff, Barrington Moore Jr (eds.), *The Critical Spirit: Essays in Honor of Herbert Marcuse* (Boston 1967)

J. Zeleny, *Die Wissenschaftslogik und das 'Kapital'* (Frankfurt 1968)

INDEX

Cambridge Studies in the History and Theory of Politics

Editor: Maurice Cowling, G. R. Elton, E. Kedourie, J. G. A. Pocock, J. R. Pole and Walter Ullmann

A series in two parts, studies and original texts. The studies are original works on political history and political philosophy while the texts are modern, critical editions of major texts in political thought. The titles include:

TEXTS

STUDIES